The

Human

Development

Experience

A psycho-social approach to human lifespan development

2nd edition

Philip B. Terry-Smith, Ph.D., Th.D.

The Human Development Experience; A psycho-social approach to human lifespan development, 2nd Edition

Photo Credit: Royalty Free Stock Photos, Microsoft clip art or Original Photography .
All original photography © 2012 PB Terry-Smith

ISBN-13   978-0-9885429-0-7 (paper back)
ISBN-13   978-0-9885429-1-4 (ebook)

Distributed by Lulu

For bulk distribution:
info@marceycreekpublishing.net

http://www.marceycreekpublishing.net

Marcey Creek Publishing™

The
Human
Development
Experience

A psycho-social approach to human lifespan development

2nd edition

Marcey Creek Publishing™

The text is for the students of human development, those path walkers who are curious about their own and other's growth. It was written primarily with the many students of substance abuse counseling programs in mind, those with whom I have had the honor of facilitating in class, those individuals who have worked their own *program* and have now committed to a lifetime of service to others.

For years, many have asked if I had a child of my own, and my response was always—no, but through years of experience working with children, youth and adults, I have raised plenty—oft times eight to ten young lives at a time. To those wonderful young people who have graced my life giving me the understanding and appreciations necessary to offer this interpretation, and that have hopefully now gone on to be great adults, and to my wonderful foster son, who has been a blessing to our household -- to my spouse and inspiration Justin—I dedicate this book, this brief look to that wondrous journey we call The Human Development Experience

About the writer

Philip Terry-Smith holds a Doctor of Philosophy degree in social systems with sub-specialties in child and adolescent development and organizational development and a Doctor of Theology degree in sacred theology. He is also completing studies for a Doctor of Laws in international humanitarian law. He has practiced in the field of human services since 1985. His specialties have included human development, organizational systems, community organizations and humanitarian care. He maintains a private practice as a professional counselor, coach and consultant and provides clinical supervision through this practice.

He serves as adjunct faculty for the graduate programs at Lincoln University of Pennsylvania and the School for Public Service Leadership, Graduate Studies at Capella University as well as for the Sociology Department of Anne Arundel Community College in Maryland and has been a featured lecturer at virtually every major university in the Baltimore/Washington Area.

For a brief time, he served as the CEO/Executive Director of Prevention Works!, a harm reduction center in DC. He also served as Executive Director, Community Development Officer for the District of Columbia office of the American Red Cross and later as the Senior Director for Emergency and International services for the National Capital Region. Prior to joining the Red Cross professional staff, he spent time as a volunteer mental health officer. In this capacity he served as a officer and supervisor at both the Pentagon and the World Trade Center, September 11th 2001 tragedies.

He holds the honor of Eagle Scout and was recognized as one of the "Outstanding Young Men of America." He is a commissioned officer with the Maryland Military Department, Maryland Defense Force and is an ordained Interfaith Chaplain.

When not working or volunteering, Dr. Terry-Smith is in studio producing music or in theatre Directing. His love for music and technical gadgetry presents an avocation for which he is quite fond and earned him the moniker "Dr. Gadget". He currently resides in Laurel, Maryland with his spouse Justin and their foster son.

Table of Contents

Introduction

The human development experience is both a fascinating and somewhat troubling study. We are faced with some of the greatest challenges and celebrate some of the greatest accomplishments. It is in fact a journey; one that began long before the *historical accident* that resulted in our conception. I call it a historical accident because regardless of one's frame of reference or beliefs about when life begins or the spiritual nature of conception, the exact moment and instance of conception is a mystery, an accidental happenstance that occurs with fertilization; the melding of a single sperm into a single egg that starts a chain of events of epic proportions.

But the journey actually began long before the historical accident. You see we are the sum total of all that has come and gone before us. In our genes is not only the genetic coding of our immediate past, our parents and grand-parents, but of our oldest ancestors and those that came before them. Science, through DNA matching, now allows us to trace our ancestry through the millennia, showing with a level of accuracy the ethnicity implicit in our family's heritage. DNA testing in the immediate can verify paternity and maternity, can identify familial genetic traits, medical vulnerabilities and other key indices of human existence.

It goes to reason then that embedded in our DNA are traits that even science is just beginning to understand. As for human development, aside from the ethnicity and ancestral legacy in our DNA, this "map" of human existence reminds us that we bear the vulnerabilities of all that has gone before us. In-fact, we are *but the sum total of all our ancestors*. With this profound assumption, we can go forward in confidence that many in our ethnic and genetic heritage have tread this path before and that we are indeed, laying the foundation for those that will follow us. Our First Nation (Native American) brothers and sisters frequently remind us in many of their teachings:

> *"In every deliberation [and action], we must consider the impact on the seventh generation... even if it requires having skin as thick as the bark of a pine."* —
> —**Great Law of the Iroquois**

Everything we do, everything we eat, drink, smoke or contract, has an impact immediately upon our being and has the strong potential to impact generations to come through the simple and often complex altering of DNA. This adds a wonderful and intriguing dimension to the human develop experience, one in which we will not venture much further into. Suffice it to say, that this journey for each of us began long ago and does not end with our final breath, but indeed will become a part of the legacy that we leave for the seventh generation and their seventh generation.

My fascination with the human development process began with what seemed like a simple academic exercise while completing studies towards a Master's degree. One of the first assignments in that curriculum was to write one's autobiography from birth to death (of course a fictional depiction from one's age at the time to end of life) and then proceed to integrate relevant developmental theory into your own personal story. For me this became much more than a "course paper". This simple exercise launched an appreciation for the intricacies of the human life journey, an appreciation for understanding this journey through the lenses of both the realm of psychology and sociology and a much deeper consideration for how we grow and mature and the influences thereon.

I welcome you to this journey—this exploration of the profound, and this discourse in the obvious—this spiritual quest and journey of your lifetime.

Theoretical Structure

For years, the forefathers of psychology and the study of human development contended that the developmental challenges ended at the period referred to as adolescence. That is once one reached puberty, cognitive, emotional, physical and social development ended. Erik Erikson, a student of Sigmund Freud through Anna Freud changed that concept, when he introduced the notion of life cycle development in an eight (later 9) stage process of psycho-social development. This text is based on the stages of psycho-social development, expanded to 11 stages as based on the work of Erikson and his contemporaries (Figure 1). It will include reference to the works of Sigmund Freud, Jean Piaget, George Herbert Mead, Charles Horton Cooley, Abraham Maslow, John Bowlby and Mary Ainsworth, and Lawrence Kohlberg as the primary theoretical framers.

An astute reader will note frequent overlaps in the "age ranges" and some discrepancy in the listed ages for a particular stage. This is because all ages listed are broad ranges as each individual develops at their own pace and rate.

There are no definitive ages for ANY of the stages just broad ranges of generalized behavior. So you will see overlap, redundancy and some out right discrepancies on the age ranges. Keep in mind that these theories were written based on statistical averages and "typical" development and behavior. Allow for a broad swath of "generally accepted and expected" behavior and tasks as you view any individual's development.

Please note here that clearly most of this framework comes from the classical theory and albeit classical, it presents from a *Eurocentric* perspective; emphasis in this text is on the relative universality of developmental stages. As found through observations and studies, regardless of society or ethnicity, we have all travelled similar paths in our development. The nuances of each culture and social order or generation presents variances, but from birth to two years old, the infant still develops the same; adolescents are adolescents faced with the same challenges whether in the communities of Washington, DC.-- in the farming fields of Ames, Iowa-- the glittery city of Los Angeles -- the mountains of Europe -- the villages of China or the townships in South

Africa. And finally, we all face the same aging and end of life challenges.

So it is offered here that for the student of human development, one must know and appreciate the classic theories and understand that all other frameworks, shaped by cultural references and ethnic nuances have evolved from the works of the original theories and concepts. Therein lies the beauty of study; this text provides you a framework by which you can delve deeper into your understanding of human development, taking these theories and this interpretation and dissecting the *truths* therein and furthering your appreciation by studying beyond what is contained here.

In this text, the term his or hers, he or she, him or her will be used interchangeably throughout to represent both sexes, genders and gender expressions.

Figure 1 Developmental stages

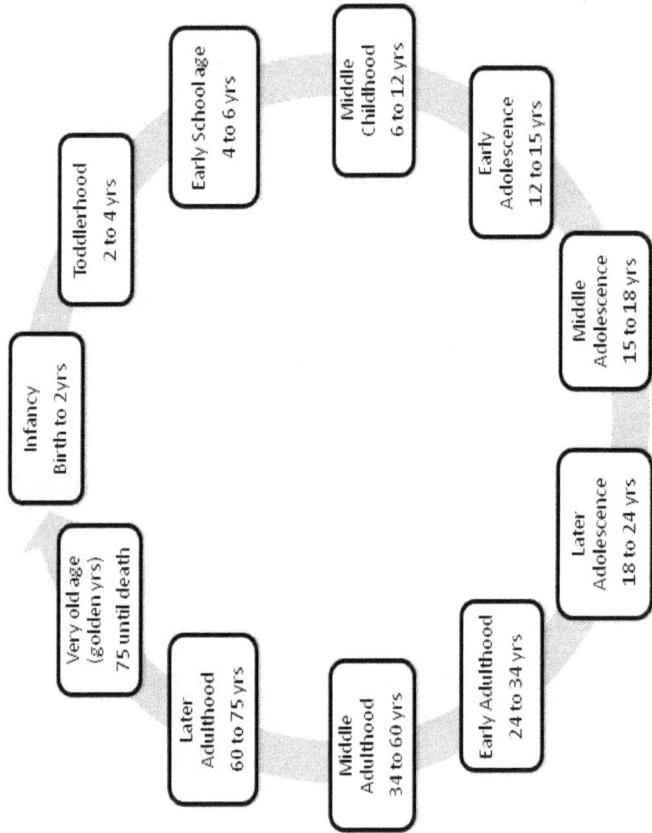

11 stages of psycho-social development based on the work of Erik Erikson

- Infancy
  Birth to 2yrs
- Toddlerhood
  2 to 4 yrs
- Early School age
  4 to 6 yrs
- Middle
  Childhood
  6 to 12 yrs
- Early
  Adolescence
  12 to 15 yrs
- Middle
  Adolescence
  15 to 18 yrs
- Later
  Adolescence
  18 to 24 yrs
- Early Adulthood
  24 to 34 yrs
- Middle
  Adulthood
  34 to 60 yrs
- Later
  Adulthood
  60 to 75 yrs
- Very old age
  (golden yrs)
  75 until death

To continue to frame the perspective of this text, we must appreciate simple definitions for psychology vs. sociology. Thus for this purpose *Psychology* is offered as the study of processes, interactions and development as related to self or internal psychodynamic development and *Sociology* as the study of processes, interactions and development as related to and with others or external social development. Further, as much of this text is based on a sociological perspective, an understanding of socialization is worthy; thus *socialization* is the universal process of becoming a member of one's society or social order. It is a continual process of indoctrination and a learning process that happens over the human life span as we age and enter new social groups.

Our developmental processes, framed through the two distinct yet related schools of thought, provide the atmosphere in which we learn language and grow to appreciate ourselves and others as distinct beings. We also develop social skills, build attachments and meaningful relationships, and learn social interactions, morals and expectations; these characteristics continue to evolve as we travel the journey of our own individual and group social development.

One final but very important word to set the tone and frame the perspective posited for healthy development; *__CHOICES__*!!! We should instill good choices and good healthy decision making from the moment a new being enters this world until the moment we exit. Always, always, always-- when considering the most important element to encourage a sound psycho-social, emotional, physical, spiritual and moral development --remember to provide as many healthy choices as possible. Even an infant in a crib can have opportunity to make choices, simply by the toys and items on the mobile hanging above them. By always providing opportunities for choice from birth, certainly in the early developmental years and most importantly in adolescence, we help to develop a strong sense of self, self worth and vitally, and significantly, an internal locus of control.

That internal locus of control is the ability to make good healthy sound decisions for oneself WITHOUT the need for someone to look over us or a threat of punitive retribution to correct poor behavior. Much of the challenges we face as a society (speaking of American society here) is that so many people grew up with the *big people* making all the choices, restricting our options and punishing us if we failed to "comply".

A child who learns that there are always choices and that is always provided with multiple choices for any given situation (including discipline) learns to respect others and that they can always find a safe, respectful and healthy way to resolve conflict. More on this later as we progress through the ages. I welcome you to what I hope will be a life long journey of learning about and appreciating the human development experience.

> "I believe that we are solely responsible for our choices, and we have to accept the consequences of every deed, word, and thought throughout our lifetime...We need to teach the next generation of children from Day One that they are responsible for their lives. Mankind's greatest gift, also its greatest curse, is that we have free choice. We can make our choices built from love or from fear."
>
> ~ *Elisabeth Kubler-Ross*

So when does it begin?

Conception to birth

As mentioned in the introduction, our journey begins with a historical accident, though the map was laid out long before and is transmitted with the DNA coding. The following images reflect the developing fetus at various stages in the typical 36 week gestation common for humans.

Figure 2 Fertilization

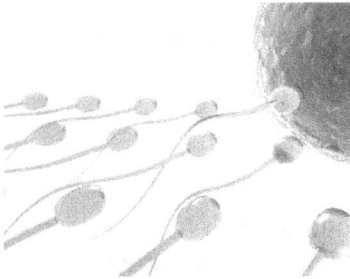

Figure 3 Embryonic Divide

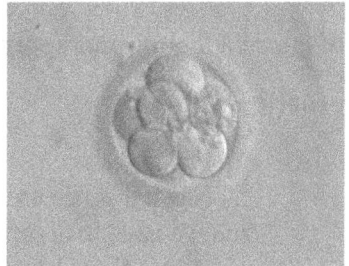

Figure 4 First trimester week 9

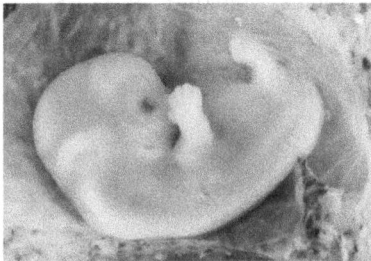

Figure 5 Second Trimester Four months post conception

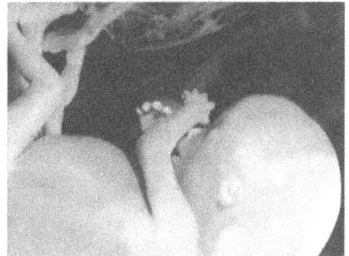

Figure 6   Second Trimester Month 5   Figure 7   Third Trimester 7 mos

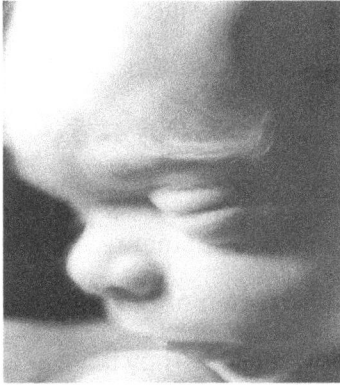

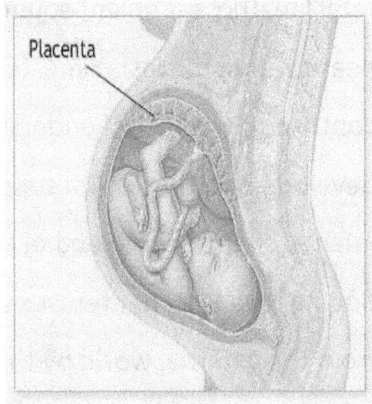

Placenta

Figure 8   Newborn

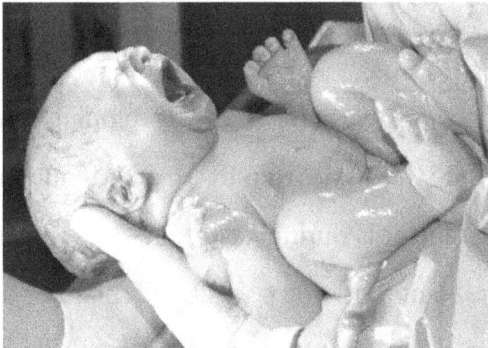

Research shows that early language skills can develop in utero-- that is before the infant is born. A study by Wermke (2009) found that not only are neonates capable of producing different cry melodies, the infant prefers to produce melody

patterns typical to the language they have heard during their fetal life, those ambient sounds and language intonations heard within the last trimester of gestation. Further, in contrast to traditional understandings of language development, these data support the importance of human infants' crying as the seed of language development. A further finding revealed that fetuses are able to memorize sounds from the external world by this last trimester. They have a particular sensitivity to melody contour of both music and language. As a result, newborns tend to prefer their mother's voice and tone over others. (Retrieved from http://www.sciencedaily.com/releases/2009/11/091105092607.htm)

I often jokingly refer to the developing fetus as a parasite. While this may seem harsh and dehumanizing, the truth of the matter is during gestation, the fetus lives off of the mother. By definition a parasite is a plant or an animal organism that lives in or on another and takes its nourishment from that other organism. What is most important about this fact relates to the overall health and wellbeing of the mother. What she takes in, the developing infant takes in. Every drink, food, intoxicant, and breathe of air has a direct impact on the developing fetus. Much is known now about the impact of alcohol and other drug consumption by a mother on the developing fetus. Less is known about the impact of certain foods, over-the-counter medications, illnesses or other un-healthy conditions and emotional states. Suffice it to say that during the pregnancy, it is imperative that the mother take special care of her body so that the fetus has a healthy environment in utero in which to begin its life journey.

Infants, Birth to 2 Years

Trust vs. Mistrust

Perhaps the most important stage in human development after that first breath is that of birth to age two. During these delicate formative years, the foundation is laid for much -- if not all -- of one's future development and social maturity. Accordingly, most theorists recognize childhood, particularly infancy as the formative stages of the personality.

Physical development during infancy stage occurs very rapidly, with significant changes and growth spurts occurring monthly. Craig (2001) suggests that at four months, an infant has doubled in weight from birth (typically from 6 to 8 pounds) and has increased on an average four inches in length. The once *crying all night* infant usually sleeps for most of the night at this point. Though some muscle strength and control is developing, the four month old is still very delicate and can be injured if handled improperly.

Figure 9   Growth and proportion 8 week gestation to age two

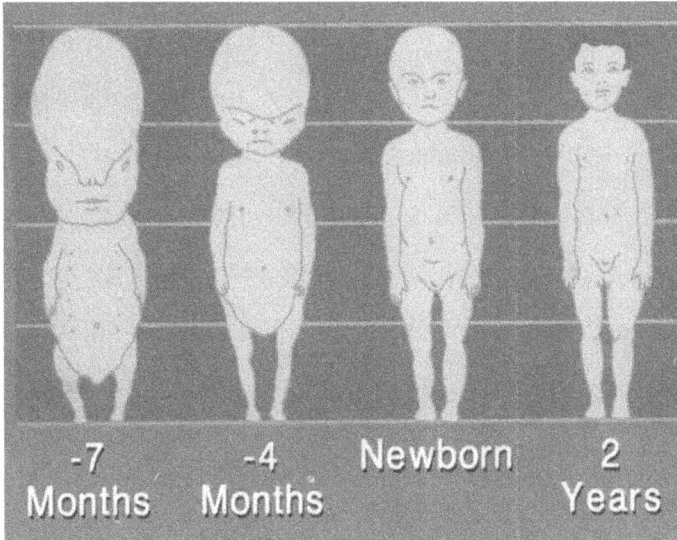

Piaget (1952) refers to the ages of birth to age 2 as the _sensorimotor stage_. This is the stage in which all learning and cognitive development occurs by the experience of the senses and involuntary (later voluntary) movement and control of muscles. During this period, the infant develops several cognitive skills by 'adapting' and 'assimilating' differing schemes. The schemes begin as simple looking, feeling, visually following, grasping and crying in early development and eventually advancing to manipulation of toys and other objects and mobility. More specifically, an infant in early development will grasp objects and attempt to mouth them.

Through these actions, the infant learns the difference between objects. Much of what the child learns at this point is merely through accident. The child will feel, see, touch or hear an object through different actions or movements. As a result of these simple actions, the infant also discovers that they can change or manipulate what is seen or heard. These skills progress with age as the infant matures.

Of course everything goes directly to the mouth. Freud dubs this age the ***oral stage*** (Birth to 18 months). During the oral stage, the child is focused on oral pleasures (sucking). The sucking instinct is a trait we are born with and is one of the first things an infant will do.

From birth to two months the infant:

- Lifts head slightly when on tummy
- Moves arms and legs randomly
- Smiles, coos, babbles
- Listens to voices and sounds

- Looks at faces, patterns, movement, light

- Loves to be touched and rocked

- Sleeps and cries often

- Uses sucking to self-calm

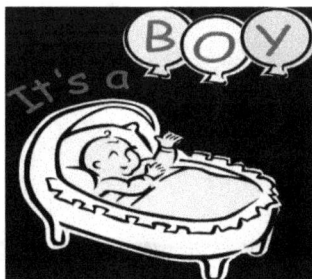

Figure 10   It's a boy

At three to four months the infant:

- Rolls from back to side and maybe from tummy to back

- Holds hands together

- Loves to play with feet

- Lifts head and chest while on tummy

- Follows you and/or activity with eyes

- Turns head in direction of sound

- Smiles

- Reach and miss/ random grab

- Fusses to be picked up

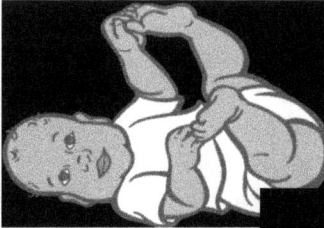

Figure 11   My toes

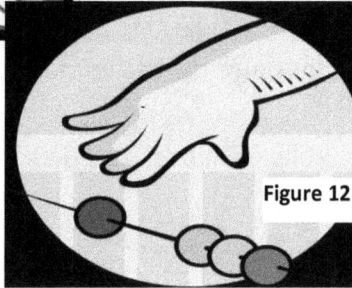

Figure 12 My Game

Behaviorally, according to Craig (2001), the four month old infant can begin to hold her head upright and can reach and grasp small objects. The grasping of small objects implies the infant has mastered some voluntary upper body muscle control and has begun to develop the ***pincher grasp***; this is a major motor skill development that allows the infant to begin to control their own environment and manipulate the physical world. The infant can also roll from stomach to back and vice-a-versa and are known to smile, coo and laugh as well.

The infant begins to examine and discover his own hands and feet. He is capable of tracing or following objects with his eyes and can perceive some colors. The baby is capable of visually distinguishing between various shapes and responds to sounds. Cognitively, the infant can remember certain objects and sounds, e.g., mother's voice and a favorite plaything. This implies the establishment of object permanence, that notion that things exist when not in one's immediate presence. This is a crucial element in the development of a sense of self and a sense of attachment to others.

It may seem a strange concept to think that infants have emotions or an emotional range, but in fact they do. ***Emotional regulation*** is a concept used to describe the variety of processes that give an infant the ability to reduce the feelings of distress and to control the intensity of their emotional state. These abilities mature over the first two years or so of life. As the infant simultaneously develops motor and cognitive skills, they also develop emotional regulation. They develop a range of techniques that can help them cope with emotional states. For newborns, the techniques might be a simple turning of the head, sucking on their hands or feet or closing their eyes. Later as the motor skills improve, the infant might move themselves away, roll over, crawl or seek other distractions to cope with emotional changes or challenges. Some of the reactions seen during this stage can be interpreted through a construct referred to as Temperament.

Temperament is the relatively stable responses to environment, stimulation and the infant's emotional self-regulation. Quite often, temperament is viewed as the physiological and biological basis of one's personality as observed in early infancy. Temperament is in fact considered a significant source of our individual differences. Temperament can be examined from three distinct aspects which include activity level, emotionality and sociability. These aspects are generally thought to derive from genetics.

Major theorists agree on three basic types of infant temperament:

- Easy
  - Regular body functions
  - Low or moderate intensity of reaction
  - Positive mood or disposition
  - Adaptability
  - Positive approach as opposed to withdrawal from new stimuli and situations
  - Active to very active
- Slow to warm
  - Tendency to withdraw from new stimuli or situations on first exposure
  - Low activity level
  - Slow to adapt
  - Low intensity of reaction to stimuli or situations
  - Somewhat negative mood or disposition

- Difficult
    - Slow to adapt to change and Unusually intense reactions
    - Irregular body functions
    - Tendency to withdraw from new stimuli or situations
    - General negative mood or disposition

An important sociological development at this stage is the development of trust. The challenge of **_trust vs. mistrust_** according to Erickson (1950) is the process through which the infant learns that their needs will be met. The infant is dependent, of course, on others (hereafter referred to as the big people) to meet all of her needs. It is no longer necessary for the mother to be 'right there'. The infant begins to accept that mother will return when she departs. The child also knows that she will be feed, that nurturing will continue and that other basic needs, such as diaper changing, will be met.

The above conditions, of course, assume that proper nurturing and care are given the infant. If the baby's basic needs: food, clothing/warmth, and comfort/nurturing are not provided, then the infant will not develop a healthy sense of trust. Most likely, the child will develop without a sense of trust of his environment or society. This is often the case with abused or neglected infants and most likely results in a failure to thrive, a condition in which the infant does not mature physically, emotionally or socially at normal rates.

Very often under the desired conditions, the infant develops trust through feeding and nurturing. When a big person holds the child for feeding (breast or bottle feeding) cuddled close, the child is comforted by the mother's warmth and touch. When the child cries, a nurturer can comfort the child by changing if necessary, or cuddling and rocking. The 'gitchie-goos' that adults are famous for giving, provides play and comfort for the crying child.

Figure 13   Mirror

At five to six months our little one:

- Begins to push up on hands and knees when on tummy

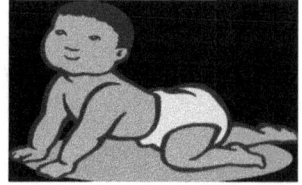

Figure 14   Crawling

- Sits by self for a short time

- Kicks

- Pincher Grasp

- Touches, grasps and bangs objects

- Sleeps through the night

Figure 15   Grasping

- Plays peek-a-boo

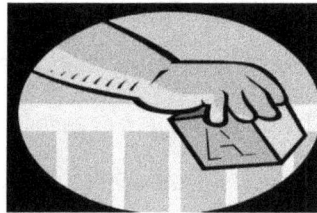

At seven to nine months, our fast developing infant:

- Crawls on hands and knees

- Pulls up to sitting and standing positions

- Stands for short periods of time holding on for support

- Grasps small objects by pinchin

- Begins some self feeding

Figure 16 Pacified Crawler

- Waves bye-bye

- Says ba-ba or ga-ga

- Plays longer with people and toys

- Enjoys other children

- Withdraws from strangers or clings to known big

Figure 17   Standing with Mom

Figure 18   Playing with the puppy

Figure 19   My bottle

By eight months, the infant has gained another four to five pounds and has grown another three to four inches. To the surprise of the breast feeding mother or an unsuspecting playmate, one or two teeth have likely developed. The infant's physical development has progressed to the point that most likely, the child can manage to get herself to a sitting position. If assisted into a standing position, the eight month old can grasp onto an object and remain standing. The infant at this stage has developed some form of mobility, though not advanced to walking; the infant can scoot or crawl.

Craig (2001), suggests that very often the eight month old is beginning to 'get into, go under and over objects'. Voluntary control over muscles is beginning to advance in development and the infant can pass objects from one hand to another and can grasp using the thumb and forefinger. This is the full development of the pincher grasp. To the dismay of the big people, this advanced muscle control a d grasping skill now allows the infant to bang two objects together and toss objects about. For the infant, this feat is exciting, amusing and can go on for long periods of time. The ability to play social games, i.e. peek-a-boo and bye bye, are developed. The infant also learns that if they drop an object, some helpful big person will pick the object up. The baby will continue with this rather 'cute' game of pick up until either the child or the big person gets bored.

The child has developed by this point a significant bond with his mother or care-giver. This first bond or attachment is perhaps one of the most significant bonds formed by humans. The development of attachments to one's care-giver in this early stage of life sets the stage for future attachments and subsequent separations. Ainsworth (1973) describes several behaviors that are indicative of an infant's bonding to a care-giver. Very often the infant will cry, laugh or make other vocalizations when in the proximity of a recognizable care-giver. The infant will also look towards the care-giver, make a movement towards him and will cling to or grasp at the care-giver if close enough.

This **_attachment_** is most likely learned from feeding and nurturing. As was previously stated, the act of feeding and nurturing is a source of solace and trust for the infant.

Having learned previously that a care-giver will attend to her, the infant attaches those feelings of comfort to the person or care-giver, thus forming a lasting bond of attachment.

By the age of eight months, infants become cautious of strangers. The infant is capable of distinguishing an unfamiliar face, voice or touch and will become uncomfortable if the stranger attempts to pick him up or handle her in any way. Craig (2001) calls this reaction ***stranger distress***. Craig states that the infant will cry in distress and will often seek the comfort of someone familiar by reaching out for them.

Speech patterns are starting to form at this age and the child is capable of repeating sounds such as mama, papa, bye-bye, na-na. The child does not understand the meaning of such sounds, but is aware that he can mimic the big people. As mentioned before, contemporary research has demonstrated that language skill acquisition can actually start in utero (before birth). The infant's perceptual preference for the surrounding language and the instinctual ability to distinguish between different languages and pitch changes are based primarily on melody and intonations familiar to the child. An infant at this stage is quite interested in and fascinated by her environment. The child does all that is within his power to explore, watch and mimic that which surrounds her.

At some point between six to twelve months the infant begins learning the process known as ***symbolic representation*** (Mandler, 1983). This process is the ability of the infant to represent something that is not physically present. For example, the infant can use gestures, sounds and other signs to represent an event or occurrence. Older infants represent sleep by resting their heads on their hands. Earlier forms that signify the development of this cognitive skill are typically demonstrated by the infant in very simple forms. An infant waving bye-bye before knowing the word or smacking lips prior to feeding are but a few examples of symbolic representation.

At the eight month stage, it is important to begin to child proof the house and infant's environment. The child's fascination with objects will lead to spilled liquids, toppled table cloths, and bumps on the head of an unwary, wandering infant. By the time the infant reaches one year, he weighs three times as much as their birth weight and has grown an additional nine or ten inches in length. In most cases the child can walk alone at this stage, or at least walk by supporting herself on a stable object.

The twelve month old has a completely developed **_pincher grasp_** (Craig, 1986) and as such has mastered the task of grasping between thumb and forefinger and can actively manipulate things around them. The child is capable of opening cabinets and drawers, can move or pull toys and can grasp hair, grass, etc. The full development of the pincher grasp also allows the child to manipulate knobs and dials. This new ability to negotiate the environment causes a very rapid introduction to limit setting. The word 'no' becomes an active part of the parent and child's vocabulary.

Figure 20 Pick up

At ten to twelve months, old our budding toddler:

- Walks holding onto furniture
- Stands alone briefly
- Finger feeds self
- Says two words besides ma-ma or da-da

- Finds objects hidden under containers (object permanence)
- Drops objects into and out of containers

The twelve month old is also learning to speak and understand (not just mimic) their first words. 'Mama', 'papa', bye –bye' and 'no-no' are frequent early vocabulary that is not just mimicked but understood. The one year old is also capable of feeding herself. The child can hold a cup or spoon and can manage quite well with bite size food portions.

Figure 21   Block Puzzle

From 13 to 15 months the little one:

- Walks alone
- Creeps up stairs
- Uses spoon to feed self
- Drinks independently from cup
- Cooperates with dressing
- Uses simple words or phrases/imitates big people words
- Begins simple pretend play
- Becomes more independent
- Refuses food
- Begins to use the word "NO" with great emphasis

As the child begins to enter the second year, a battle of wills often ensues as the child tests new found abilities and language. The child will sometimes refuse foods previously liked, will refuse to go to bed and will cry and throw a temper tantrum when told to do or stop doing something. With the refusal of food, a knowing parent will be wise to observe closely to see if it is simply limit testing or whether it is an early indication of a food allergy.

Figure 22 In my mouth mom?

Figure 23 Stacked blocks

Figure 24 Car roll

Figure 25 Spooky, big and strong

The 16 to 18 month old:

- Runs swiftly
- Walks up steps (with rail or hand held)
- Begins to throw ball using whole arm
- Feeds self with spoon
- Takes of simple clothing
- Says six to ten words
- Loves simple puzzles, scribbling and imitation games

By the age of two, the child developed his cognitive skills to the point of 'imitation' according to Piaget (1952). This new skill manifests in play. The child learns to imitate the actions of others and often practices these skills in play.

Brushing teeth, drinking from cups, using eating utensils, etc. are examples of this new found behavior. The development of object permanence or the ability to realize that an object continues to exist even though it is out of sight solidifies between eighteen and twenty-four months. Piaget (1952) asserts however, that an infant does not develop a full sense of object permanence until they begin to search for hidden objects such as misplaced toys.

Figure 26 No Mommy

Figure 27 Building Blocks

Our two year old wonder child:

- Jumps with both feet off floor
- Throws and kicks ball
- Walks up and down steps
- Puts on simple clothing
- Matches objects by color
- Speaks more clearly and in short sentences
- Points to body parts

- Throws periodic temper tantrums
- Plays alongside other children

Although these skills manifest in simpler forms as mentioned earlier (as early as five or six months) they are not fully developed until about age two. All of these seemingly simple skills are profoundly important to the developing child as each skill layers to further learning. Each task opens new neuro-pathways in the brain. Mead (2001) contends that from birth to age two, the child is egocentric and rightfully so. This helps the child learn about his world in relationship to self. How does this body work and how does it fit in this 'new' place and how does this 'new' world work?

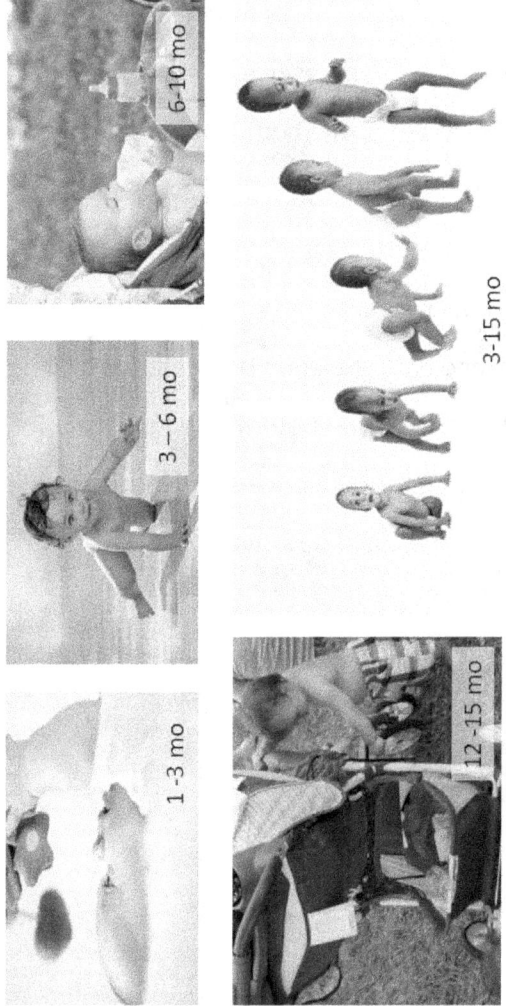

Infant to toddler motorskill development

Figure 28 Motorskill development

Toddler 2 to 4 years old

Autonomy vs. shame or doubt

Upon entering the toddler stage at age two or three, the infant is walking quite well on her own. The stance is wide armed and unsteady but the toddler can maneuver. The toddler can climb, pull or push and can hang by their hands and can grasp objects strongly with both hands. By age three, the infant can run and walk with their feet closer together, thus establishing a better gate. The three year old starts to establish a preference for their right of left hand. They extend the preferred hand for grasping offered items, i.e.; bottles, cookies, toys etc.

Whereas a two or three year old may still be experiencing some difficulty in the coordination of movements, a four year old has virtually mastered physical motor skills. She is capable of jumping (standing broad jump), varying the speed and direction while running. Typical four year olds can negotiate large pencils or crayons and can begin to draw somewhat discernible patterns. (Gesell, 1940)

Freud relates the ages of 2 to 4 as the ***anal stage***. In this stage child's focus of pleasure is on eliminating and retaining feces and waste. Through society's pressure, mainly via parents, the child has to learn to control anal stimulation and elimination—the potty training period.

Gesell (1940) also suggests that three or four year olds can also negotiate buttons through a button hole and that by age five, the youngster can manage zippers and may be able to tie his own shoes. By age four, a toddler can begin to manipulate drawing and painting material in such a way as to create an actual drawing or painting. Further, the four year old can also build or design structures, i.e.; houses, buildings, etc., as opposed to the more 'abstract' structures of three year old.

Cognitively, the toddler has become an active learner seeking out answers to things in her environment. In doing so, the toddler is beginning to develop his own sense of the world and reality. Though the toddler has not developed a sense of time or numbers, and certainly has not developed a sense of cause and effect, she has begun, by age five, to lay the foundations for future cognition. By this age, the toddler has progressed in language from speaking one word or phrases to complete sentences and questions. The toddler also experiences his knowledge through symbols. Likewise, objects are defined by their functions and or properties.

Erikson (1950) suggests that toddlers are developing a sense of _**autonomy vs. shame**_ or doubt. As such, the child tests various experiences. The toddler tests her self- control (in play and interactions with others) and through his actions, learn that he can control certain aspects of his environment. Through these tests, the child learns that much of their actions are self-controlled as opposed to control by others. If the child receives positive feedback or reactions to her actions, a sense of autonomy will begin to develop. Likewise, negative feedback could result in shame or doubt in ones abilities. Kindergarten and preschool are vital in the development of autonomy, as the structure of those programs allow for exploration and free play.

Piaget (1952), in his pre-operational developmental stage (ages 2-7), shares that the child is engaged in language acquisition and learning through observing the actions an operations of the big people. He notes that children in this stage cannot yet understand concrete logical patterns and cannot mentally manipulate data and information further he suggest that the child is unable to take understand the point of view of others, which he termed egocentrism. During the preoperational stage, the child becomes increasingly skilled at using symbols, evidenced by the increase in playing and pretending.

As shown in Figure 29, the child in the pre-operational stage observes closely as his older sibling builds the snow man. The pre-operational toddler can tell you precisely how to construct a snow man but it will be very sequential and her understanding of the process must follow the precise pattern observed. Any deviation from that pattern and the toddler cannot understand and thus the symbol (in this case the snowman) is incorrect or not accurate. Mead (2001), offers that the period of ages 2 -5 (encompassing the toddler years) is the ***imitation stage***. He calls it such because the child learns by imitating _everything_ the big people do. Do note here the emphasis on _everything_; what the child observes, they will imitate and attempt to do. It is through such imitation that the child develops a greater appreciation of symbols and actions.

Figure 29 Pre-operational thought

Our three to four year old can:

- feed himself (with some spilling)

- know what is food and what is not food

- hold a crayon well

- build a tower of 54 blocks

- substitute one object for another in pretend play (as in pretending a block is a "car")

- throw a ball overhead

- open doors

- understand "I," "you," "he," and "she"

- believe everything centers around him ("if I hide my eyes, no one will see me")

Figure 30 Toddlers at play

- answer whether she is a boy or girl match objects that have same function (as in putting a cup and plate together)
- count 2 to 3 objects
- hold a glass in one hand
- wash and dry hands by himself
- fold paper, if shown how
- try to catch a large ball)
- laugh at silly ideas (like "milking" a dog)
- recognize sounds in the environment
- avoid some dangers, like a hot stove or a moving car
- look through a book alone

Figure 31 Toddlers in playground

- walk up steps, alternating feet
- understand what "1" is
- ask to use the toilet almost every time
- enjoy being read to
- talk about feelings and mental states (e.g., remembering)
- dress herself with help
- put on shoes (but not tie laces
- use the toilet with some help
- remember what happened yesterday
- pay attention for about 3 minutes
- jump with both feet
- understand "now," "soon," and "later"
- use 3-5 word sentences
- ask short questions
- repeat simple rhymes
- match circles and squares
- match an object to a picture of that object
- walk on tiptoes if shown how
- know some numbers (but not always in the right order)

- walk in a straight line
- know where things usually belong
- play spontaneously with two or three children in a group
- assign roles in pretend social play ("You be mommy;" "I be daddy")
- kick a ball forward
- pedal a tricycle
- demonstrate some shame when caught in a wrongdoing
- try to make others laugh
- follow simple one-step commands
- use plurals ("dogs," "cars," "hats")
- name at least 10 familiar objects
- name at least one color correctly
- imitate housework or help with simple tasks
- know her first and last name

Figure 32 Toddler skills

Figure 33 Toddler experience

Early school ages 4 to 6 years old

Initiative vs. guilt

As the child enters day-care, pre-school or kindergarten, she learns through play and learning exercises and begins to explore the world beyond what is in her immediate environment. Just as he develops a sense of autonomy, the child begins to develop initiative. Accordingly, Erikson (1950) calls this stage ***initiative vs. guilt***. He suggests that in the initiative vs. guilt stage, the child explores self-directed actions and consequences. Through these explorations, the child learns to determine if his actions will have a desirable or undesirable effect.

The toddler stage is also a period in which the child cognitively experiences separation and loss. Often the first real separation issues arise for the child and their parent when the youngster first enters day-care, preschool or kindergarten. For the child and the parent in many cases, entering school presents the first time a separation for any long period of time occurs. This is a traumatic experience for both. The child often protests leaving the parent and the parent often feels quite despondent when they must leave the child. The child however, will usually quickly overcome the initial shock as she becomes involved with other children.

Mead (2001) contends that by building on the imitation stage, a child between 5 and 7 enters the ***play stage***. Think of "play" on this context as not only the play of a child but the "play" of theatre. In a theatrical "play" one learns a script and acts according to the script *and* the direction of the "director" or in this instance, *the big person* with whom the child is modeling.

Freud believed that the ***phallic stage*** (age three to six) is the stage in which the pleasure zone switches to the genitals. During this stage, he asserts, boys develop unconscious sexual desires for their mother. Because of this, the boy becomes rivals with his father and sees him as competition for the mother's affection. During this time, boys also develop a fear that their father will punish them for these feelings, such as by castrating them. This group of feelings is referred to as the as ***Oedipus complex***, after the Greek Mythology figure who accidentally killed his father and married his mother. In later years Freudian contemporaries added that girls go through a similar situation, developing unconscious sexual attraction to their father. Although Freud Strongly disagreed with this, it has been termed the ***Electra complex*** by his contemporaries more recently.

By age four, the not so little one can now:

- want to know what will happen next
- follow three instructions given at one time ("Put the toys away, wash your hands, come eat.")
- distinguish between the real world and the imaginary or pretend world
- understand taking turns and can do so without always being reminded

Figure 34 School age activity

- understand "big," "little," "tall," "short"
- feed herself (with little spilling)
- try to use a fork
- hold a pencil
- try to write name
- pour from a small pitcher
- use the toilet alone

Figure 35 Learning

- ask direct questions ("May I?" "Would you?")
- want explanations of "why" and "how"
- build a tower of 7-9 blocks
- put together a simple puzzle of 4-12 pieces
- use regular past tenses of verbs ("pulled," "walked")
- use "a," "an," and "the" when speaking

- sort by shape or color

- recognize red, yellow, and blue

- count up to 5 objects

- identify situations that would lead to happiness, sadness, or anger

- draw a face

Figure 36 The "Play"

- try to cut paper with blunt scissors

- draw with the arm and not small hand movements

- completely undress herself if wearing clothes with simple fasteners

- have a large vocabulary and use good grammar often

- catch a bouncing ball

- draw a circle

- brush teeth with help

- try to skip

- sometimes unbutton buttons

- enjoy rhyming and nonsense words

- often talk about action in conversation ("go," "do," "make")

- try to buckle, button, and lace, even though she probably needs help

- act out elaborate events which tell a story (as in serving an imaginary dinner or going on a "dragon hunt")

- sometimes cooperate with other children

Figure 37 The group

- often prefer playing with other children to playing alone, unless deeply involved in a solitary task
- help clean up toys at home or school when asked to
- like to play "dress up"
  pretend to play with imaginary objects
- walk downstairs using a handrail and alternating feet
- change the rules of a game as he goes along
- try to bargain ("I'll give you this toy if you'll give me that one")
- swing, starting by himself and keeping himself going
- like to do things for himself
- know her age and the town where she lives
- act as though a doll or stuffed animal thinks and feels on its own
- relate a simple experience she has had recently
- understand "next to"
- share when asked
- enjoy tag, hide-and-seek and other games with simple rules

Bowlby (1969), suggests that the child at this point develops an extended sense of attachment. She learns that there is a home base, e.g.; mom will be there when he returns from school. Accordingly, the relationship between the big person and the child undergoes a gradual change. The big person becomes more of a consultant for the child. The child is no longer dependent on physical proximity but begins instead to depend on symbolic representation or re-enactment to help reaffirm attachment. The child learns to talk with the big person and share experiences in an attempt to re-create the feelings while striving to reaffirm the bond.

Figure 38 Concrete thinking

Figure 39 Make Believe

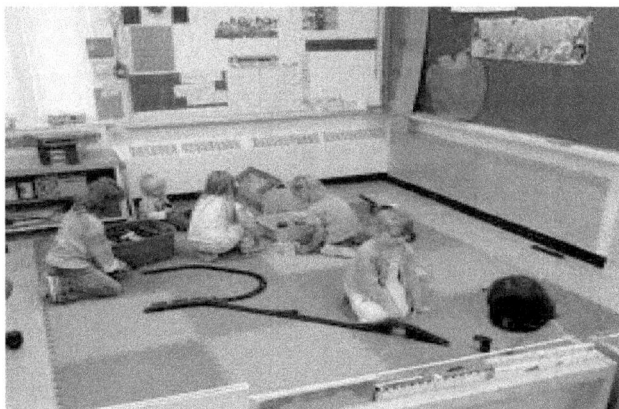

Middle Childhood-School ages 6-12

Industry vs. Inferiority

As the child enters the mid-childhood or pre-adolescent stage, he begins to develop more concrete concepts. Known as the ***concrete operations stage*** (Piaget, 1952), the youngster begins to understand time and distance, can weigh objects, and can visualize complex sequential operations. Principles and concepts at this stage are only understood in the concrete. During this time, children gain a better understanding of mental operations. They begin to think logically about concrete events, but have difficulty understanding abstract or hypothetical concept. They understand through hands-on experiments.

Children at this stage of concrete operations are good with the use of inductive logic which involves going from a specific experience to a general principle. Conversely, they have difficulty using deductive logic that may involve using a general principle to determine the outcomes. Of particular note during the development of concrete operations is the understanding of reversibility, or awareness that actions can be reversed. An example of this is being able to reverse the order of relationships between categories. For example, a child might be able to recognize that her dog is a poodle, that a poodle is a dog, and that a dog is an animal and vise-a-versa.

In the earlier years of this stage (7, 8, 9 years old) sexuality is generally repressed. The child usually experiences a stage of natural *homo-social* attractions which has little to do with sexuality as we think of it as adults; significant sexual relationships at this stage are usually not common. This stage implies an attraction and affinity to <u>social activities</u> and <u>social attraction</u> to *perceived* like gender i.e.; little boys want to be with and play with little boys and little girls want to be with and play with little girls. Freud refers to this as the ***latency stage*** (age six to puberty). It's during this stage that sexual urges remain repressed and children interact and play mostly with same sex peers.

The child is generally well into school by this point and through school and play, has refined sensorimotor skills and intellectual abilities. Erikson (1950) titles this pre-adolescent stage as industry vs. inferiority. The child experiences failure and competence through the feedback of others. The quality of her performance is now judged and rated (school performance reports) and their peers can now judge them, often harshly through teasing and intimidation. The child is integrated into a more complex society through peer groups and classes (school). Additionally, the child also begins to develop more complex roles and identities during this stage. Competition of family vs. others in society emerges. It is typical in childhood teasing to profess that "my father is better than your father", etc.

Mead refers to this stage as ***the game***. This stage is epitomized as the stage at which we learn what are the rules and how do I play this and how to master the game...this

Figure 40 Going to School

Figure 41 Thinking Through

Figure 42 Beginning to reason

So, our little one has definitely grown quite a bit by this point. Their bodies have taken on new shapes and forms and shortly a whole new experience will soon begin! (Figure 43)

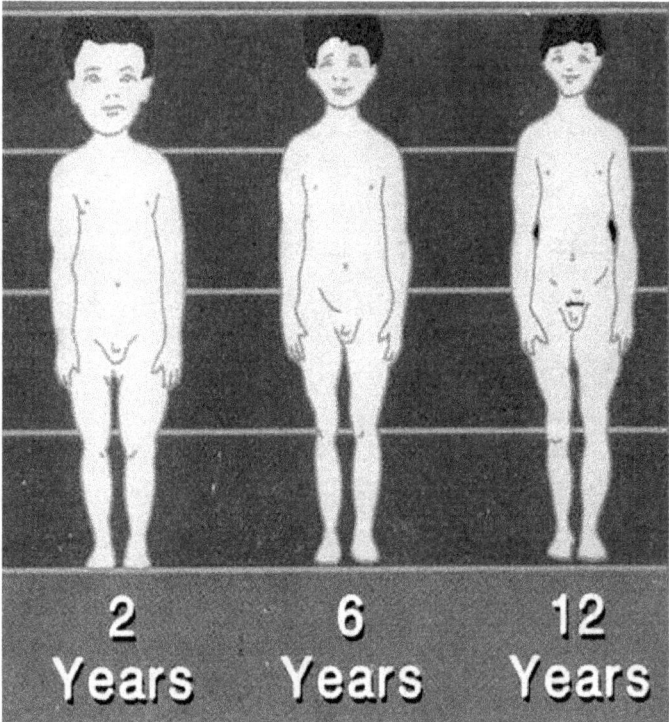

Figure 43 The changing child's body

The Primary Functions of Caregivers

So while our little one has gone off to school and is beginning to establish some level of independence, there have been some substantial responsibilities on the shoulders of *the big people*. I'll refer to these as the Primary Functions of Caregivers.

The **first** ***primary function*** of the caregivers is to be the:

- Architect of the child's world

    - With the Tasks of :

        - Creating a safe, accessible, caring and stimulating environment

        - Introducing challenges appropriately

    - Benefits to child of such care include:

        - encouraged curiosity and creativity

        - Development of self esteem

        - Development of a sense of mastery and competence

Similar to an "architect" that designs a structure, the primary caregiver in the architect roles designs the structure and physical environment in which the developing child can safely explore, grow and learn. This includes perhaps going out of the way to insure safety, locks on cabinets, capping open electrical outlets, installing safety gates etc. It also requires a plethora of child-safe toys, games and items so the child is free to choose what to play with and when. The providing of a stimulating and accessible environment cannot be underestimated for the curious child is one that will quest for knowledge, another one of those skills like decisions making that we want to instill from birth.

The **second primary function** is to be the:

- Consultant

    - The core task is to :

        - Teach and explain about the physical and social worlds

        - Respond appropriately to excitement, frustration, pain, anger

        - Give help when needed (and asked!)

    - Benefits to child:

        - reinforces curiosity and the excitement of learning

        - Develops problem solving skills and abilities

- Encourages confidence and self reliance, but with awareness of limitations

- Learning to trust and rely on others

Good consultants observe, recommend, model and teach, but recognize the independence and abilities of the entity in which they are consulting, in this case, the child. Children really are quite independent, obviously creative and curious and can and will solve challenges on their own, but as this whole adventure is new to them, they sometimes require someone with a bit more experience to help explain or teach. Even the youngest toddler can express frustration and will 'hold something up' to *the big person* when they need assistance. Acknowledge this frustration and request and wait for it, wait for the child to struggle for a bit then for them to ask you (demonstrate a desire for your help) by reaching up to you for assistance.

The **final primary function** is that of the Authority. Now we're not talking authority for authority's sake or necessarily authority "over" the child though we all know the big person ultimately is "over" the child. I'm talking the reasoned authority that sets boundaries for safe growth and development. The authority in this case is

— Tasked with:

- Developing clear expectations

- Setting limits

- Responding consistently to child's behavior

- Rewarding and disciplining appropriately

— Benefits to child:

- Learning to take responsibility for his/her own actions

- Develops self esteem

- Develops internal social controls

- Develops awareness of and sensitivity to the needs of others

Authority should not be confused with discipline or that of "punishment" (which will be discussed a little later; this merely refers to the means of establishing boundaries, helping to instill discipline and developing an ***internal locus of control.*** An internal locus of control is what will allow a child, then teen then adult to make reasoned decisions and "right" decisions when faced with conflict, challenge or moral dilemma. Such decisions should be made as we mature without the fear of retribution or "punishment" as the "*big people*" will not always be there to make those decisions for us. Like decision making and a quest for knowledge, the

building of an internal locus of control shaped by the afore-
mentioned three primary functions can begin at birth and be
fostered and developed throughout the human lifespan,
especially in the formative years. Trust when I say, you want
to spend time on this when the child is still a little one or by
the time they become teens, you will certainly wish you did!

The referencing the tasks of the primary caregiver
here in relationship to raising a young one, as one matures
and grows, those care giver tasks change to reflect the
appropriate developmental stage. Caregivers will find
themselves exercising similar tasks when they are in a
position to care for their elders, parents and those in the later
stages of life.

Discipline

Discipline differs from punishment in that it teaches
and encourages children to learn from their mistakes rather
than suffering for them. Punishment typically takes
something away, restricts in some form or at the extreme, is
delivered in some physical or corporal form such as a
spanking or at worst a beating. There is much data to
establish just how ineffective physical punishment is and how
physical punishment goes hand-in-hand in establishing a
culture of violence and/or physical abuse. While there is

certainly debate about the use of corporal punishment, there is consensus that imposing suffering actually shifts the focus from the lesson that needs to be learned to who is in control. As a result, punishment focuses on the parent being responsible for controlling a child's behavior, rather than the child controlling his/her own behavior, which is the focus of discipline.

The difference then between discipline and punishment is huge. The proper application of discipline or rather the lack thereof goes a very long way in creating self control, self discipline, integrity, respect and sound ethical balance. If this were easy, we would not have discipline problems with large numbers of teens in our schools and community; of course it is not, it takes practice and above all **PATIENCE!** Now *"big people"* get this mucked up all the time. I'm not talking "Dr. Spock" here, in fact positive discipline doesn't need any punishments at all; once you've got the child wanting to please you and used to a lovely relationship with you, they want to keep it like that. Some key points on *discipline vs. punishment*

- **Discipline:**

    - Teaches a child how to act.

    - Should make sense to a child.

    - It should have something to do with what he has done wrong.

- Helps a child feel good about himself.

- It gives him the chance to correct his mistakes.

- It puts him in charge of his actions.

- Develops an ***internal locus of control***

- **Punishment:**

   - Only tells a child that she is bad.

   - It does not tell a child what she should do instead.

   - May not make sense to the child as it is typically given with a delay or out-of-context.

   - Usually has nothing to do with what the child did wrong.

   - Requires constant enforcement and ***external control*** by the big people

So what works:

- Just showing your displeasure is enough to keep things on track.

- Once you've got that positive relationship, you shouldn't need punishments at all.

- Punishments should be an absolute last resort in any discipline method.

Adolescence 12-24 years old

Identity vs. Identity Confusion
Puberty to please move out!

At age 12 or there about, the youth enters adolescence. He has experienced significant physical growth spurts which are often sporadic and awkward. The marker of adolescence is the onset of puberty, which occurs at different ages. This is signified by significant physical changes coupled with emotional and hormonal (body chemistry) changes and is often a source of great distress for the adolescent and his parent. For the adolescent, puberty brings on new sensations and feelings. For young ladies, puberty brings about a start in the menstrual cycle, the development of breast and body hair. Some young ladies can begin this stage as early as age 9. For young men, their muscles begin to develop and take on more definition; he too develops body hair, his genitals enlarge and he begins to produce/release ejaculate (semen). Very often, young men begin this process a year or two after their female counter parts, a source of scorn and ridicule at school.

The rapid physical changes for adolescents cause a period of awkwardness. Muscle control is often retarded as the youth adjusts to arms that are suddenly too long or legs and feet that have all of a sudden outgrown the rest of his body. Parents are frustrated at the constant need for new clothing as one size may only fit the youth for a month or two.

The identity crisis, synonymous with adolescence, develops from a variety of sources. Erikson (1950) distinguishes this stage ***Identity vs. role confusion/diffusion stage***. He asserts that the adolescent (particularly in Western society) must develop a coherent sense of identity out of a variety of separate roles. These roles include: child, student, son or daughter, role model (for younger siblings), young adult and for many young Americans –parent. The key question at this stage is "who am I?" From this search for identity, the youngster must find basic values and attitudes and must reconcile and integrate these 'new' values and attitudes into a coherent sense of self without conflict.

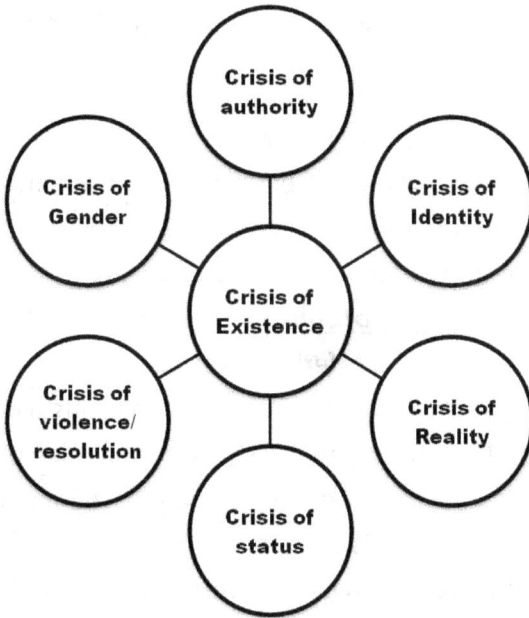

Figure 44 Seven Crises of Adolescence

As if the adolescent were not challenged enough with simply understanding and reconciling their identity, they are faced with several other challenges along the way. In a concept modeled on the work of R. McCleary, I offer for you the notion of seven crises (Figure 44) that each adolescent must overcome in the process of refining their identity. I would contend that these challenges occur simultaneously with the adolescent developmental stage and do not necessarily occur in any particular order, but that each must be overcome. What we also know is that many youth do not overcome these, and unfortunately the "crisis of existence" presents the most troubling issues. The rate of suicide and overt risk taking behavior among teens speaks volumes to this issue.

Let's take a closer look at the seven crises; the first is the ***crisis of authority***. Think back to our conversation on the *Tasks of Primary Caregivers*, one of those tasks was that of Authority. In that I mentioned we are striving to instill and build an ***internal locus of control.*** So when referring to the crisis of authority, I am offering that this crisis is the first time the budding adolescent is challenged with facing a decision to act in a certain manner. Previously, the young person could rely on *the big people* to render decision or to immediately correct behavior or actions. As a teen, *the big people* are not always around; teens have more independence and must rely on internal control to make decisions. Of course this goes without saying that adults must do this all the time. For teens it is learned and the first time they have that profound experience of making a sound decision, they face, even if minor, the ***crisis of authority***.

The ***crisis of identity*** is perhaps the hallmark of this stage of development. It is the primary task of adolescence. Up to this point in life, the "big people" have told us who we are, what we believe and have shaped our identity and perception of ourselves. As we move into middle to late adolescents, we have the task of establishing an identity that is separate from that of our parents. In cognitive development, we are shifting from Piaget ***concrete operations*** to that of ***formal operations*** or the ability to abstract. This change of thinking allows us to project outside of the routine or concrete thought. We can for the first time experience the world as a unique and separate entity from our parents. Our interactions with peers and larger social groups help us to shape and understand who we are.

The ***crisis of reality*** comes as we begin to shift our perspective of whom and what we are. Up until our *tween* years, those magickal years at the tail end of childhood (around 10-12 y/o) our world view was shaped the big people and as our cognition or thinking was limited to concrete operations, we had little opportunity to experience or challenge that perspective. As we mature and grow in adolescence, one of the significant shifts is the move to formal operational thought, the ability to abstract and think through processes. So the "wise tales", fairy tales and mythology that *the big people* gave to us as toddlers and young children start to fade.

The tween and early teen years also presents perhaps

the first time we are exposed to culture, races, lifestyle, social, and economic statuses that

Figure 45   Teen Status   may be grossly different from what we know. If you remember that elementary schools are by nature very homogenous as they typically draw from a rather small neighborhood cluster, while middle or junior high school have a wider swath of a jurisdiction and high schools even wider. For the first time in our lives, we may be confronted with the reality of our family and how that reality is different from the reality of others that we are now in contact with -- our peers. Reconciling who we are and what we are brings us resolution of this crisis.

I will offer the sociological definition of status to shed light on the **_crisis of status._** In that form, status is a social or professional position, condition, or standing to which varying degrees of responsibility, privilege, and esteem are attached. Further it is the relative position or standing of a person or thing in a society or order. As we reconciled our **_reality_**, we faced our status. The relative economics of our family, our race, culture, religion and where those variables sit in the hierarchy and stratification of our society come to focus. There are two forms a status that applies. The first is our **_acquired status_**. The acquired status is the status in which we were born. For example; I was born an African/Native American male to a teen mother in a lower/ middle class community in a working class city. The acquired status _just is_. In some cultures, acquired status pre-determines your opportunity or lack thereof in life and it is simply the place you will always hold.

Now one's ***achieved status*** is status that one works for
of their own volition. Achieved status can be upward,
downward or lateral movement or mobility and can change,
for better or worse, ones "place" in their society. Using myself
as an example again—though my acquired status was as
stated above, I have ***achieved*** a higher social standing by the
nature of the academic achievements (multiple doctorates),
professional positions (having served as a CEO, being an
ordained chaplain and member of clergy, and Military Officer)
and relative economic stability (home owner). These are all
things that I have accomplished which in my society, places
me at a different status from that in which I was born.

On the other hand, I could have followed the path that
many peers who lived and grew up in the same neighborhood
as I; all had the same or strikingly similar "acquired status" but
very different "achieved status". Many from *the old
neighborhood* have moved *down* the social ladder, having not
gone to further education, being perpetually un- or under-
employed or for some, having fallen prey to addiction and/or
criminal activity. So resolving this crisis requires an
acceptance of one's acquired status and some commitment to
achieve a different status—good, bad or indifferent—in
adolescence, we map out the path we will take towards our
own achieved status.

The ***crisis of violence/resolution***: For most of us,
somewhere in our early childhood we learned that we should
not hit others, or at the very least to not hit unless someone

hits you first (self-defense). Of course, *the big people* in our lives where there to enforce such restraint (in most cases)! As we grow we learn along with social skill, how to resolve issues, use words to express our feelings and that violence is not an acceptable option for resolving conflict. This notion of peaceful resolution is predicated on living in violence free environment. For a child that grows in a violent environment, they learn that violence is the only means to resolve conflict. That child becomes a violent teen or young adult and in some cases may actually develop sociopathic tendencies.

Now this is not to say that all children exposed to violence will become sociopathic and likewise some children exhibit sociopathic tendencies when raised in seemingly "ideal" environments. One thing we know for sure, children who experience domestic violence or abuse are likely to become abusers themselves. In-fact –

> The child may also develop an understanding that it is normal to be in an abusive relationship. For boys, especially, the danger is great that they will become abusers themselves. Boys from homes where domestic violence occurs have up to a ten times greater chance of abusing their partner than girls. Domestic violence tends to become more intense over time, and its effects can seriously interrupt normal emotional and physical development for children – even perpetuating a cycle of abuse for generations. (Retrieved from: http://www.elementsbehavioralhealth.com/mental-health/domestic-violence-perpetuates-cycle-of-abuse-in-children/)

The ***crisis of gender*** The World Health Organization offers a definition of gender as being the result of socially constructed ideas about the one's behavior, actions, and the roles a particular sex performs. It is further defined as the beliefs, attitude, and values assumed and exhibited by individuals within the parameters of their society. Now most importantly, this should _not_ be confused with sex, sexual identity, or sexual orientation. These will be defined and explored later. To the contrary, gender represents what it *means* to be a man or a woman in a given society and what the society expects from that man or woman. Do not think that the gender roles and gender expectation are universal. There are some societies where what we think of as expectations for men and women are completely reversed from that here in the U.S.

We tend to think of clothing or outward appearance as a demarcation of gender. For example, men wear pants and "masculine" clothing and women wear dresses and "feminine" clothing. Doing so will certainly get us in trouble. There are thousands of "exceptions" to what a given society expects for dress and appearance. Length of hair, earrings or other jewelry adornments, long

Figure 46   Gender Confusion

flowing open garments, pants like garments, skirt like garments, and body hair are but a few of the outward appearance markers that vary greatly amongst and within societies. Expectations for nurturance of children or for the primary "provider" also greatly vary.

So this ***crisis of gender*** is all about the adolescent discovering and reconciling for themselves what being a man or a woman means in their society and whether that social construct is congruent with their own psychological and physiological self- perception and self reality. It would take another entire book to fully explain the concept of gender Identity and I certainly encourage further study of this rather complex and challenging topic. For our purposes here, it will suffice to say that our adolescent is faced with becoming comfortable with their own gender and gender expression and how that plays out in terms of the new found identity, the emerging sexual identity and the evolving sexuality.

We actually start the program of gender expectation pre-birth; we do it by the clothing we buy infants, the toys we give the child, the words we use, etc. Of the most harmful, in my opinion are words to the effect of "you are just like your father/mother" then in the next breath an articulation of some disparaging comment or fault, or less than desirable quality of the parent the child is being compared to. So now the child has this "negative programming" of what is to be a "man" like his "father" or "woman" like her mother.

The *__crisis of existence__* is the final crisis faced by teens and sadly in many cases it does become _the_ final crisis. For so many of our youth as they struggle to master these crises and to build a sense of identity, they do not see the "light at the end of the proverbial tunnel" and opt for suicide, suicide by aggression or turn to alcohol, drugs and extremely risky and promiscuous sexual activity.

Figure 47 Depressed Teen

The statistics for youth suicide are alarming. Suicide is the sixth leading cause of death among 5-14 year olds and the third leading cause of death amongst 15-24 year olds. Statistically, between the mid-1950s and the late 1970s, the suicide rate among females ages 15-24, the rate more than doubled during this period (from 2.0 to 5.2) Among U.S. males between ages 15-24 more the rate than tripled (from 6.3 per 100,000 in 1955 to 21.3 in 1977). Between 1980 and 1996, the suicide rate for African-American males between ages 15-19 also doubled. These statistics are alarmingly high in all contemporary measures.

There are numerous risk factors for suicide among the young which include suicidal thoughts, psychiatric disorders (such as depression, impulsive aggressive behavior, bipolar disorder, certain anxiety disorders), drug and/or alcohol abuse and previous suicide attempts, with the risk increased if there is situational stress and access to firearms. When these startling statistics are viewed in context of the seven crises we have good cause to be alarmed.

(Retrieved from
http://www.afsp.org/index.cfm?fuseaction=home.viewpage&page_id=050
fea9f-b064-4092-b1135c3a70de1fda)

Figure 48 Teen Angst

These challenges are magnified many times over if the young person is also challenging sexuality, sexual identity, sexual orientation or gender identity. According to a report from the Centers for Disease Control and Prevention (CDC),

"Negative attitudes toward gays, lesbians, bisexuals, and transgender (LGBT) people put LGBT youth at increased risk for experiences with violence, compared with other students. Violence can include behaviors such as bullying, teasing, harassment, physical assault, and suicide-related behaviors."

(Retrieved from
http://www.cdc.gov/lg
bthealth/youth.htm)

In a survey released by the CDC in 2009 survey of more than 7,000 LGBT middle and high school students aged 13–21 years found that in the past year, because of their sexual orientation—

- Four out of ten had been physically harassed at school;
- Six out of ten felt unsafe at school; and
- Eight out of ten students had been verbally harassed at school;
- And one in five had been the victim of a physical assault at school.

Figure 49   Gay Youth

Further, as alluded to above, LGBTQ youth are also at increased risk for suicidal thoughts and behaviors, suicide attempts, and suicide. A national sample survey of adolescents in grades 7–12 found that LGBTQ youth were more than twice as likely to have attempted suicide as their heterosexual peers. In another survey of more than 7,000-- 7th and 8th graders from a large Midwestern county examined the effects of school climate and homophobic bullying on lesbian, gay, bisexual, transgendered and questioning (LGBTQ) youth.

That survey revealed that --

- Students who were questioning their sexual orientation reported more bullying, homophobic victimization, unexcused absences from school, drug use, feelings of depression, and suicidal behaviors than either heterosexual or LGBTQ students;
- LGBTQ youth were more likely than heterosexual youth to report high levels of bullying and substance use; and
- LGBTQ students who did not experience homophobic teasing reported the lowest levels of depression and suicidal feelings of all student groups (heterosexual, LGBT, and questioning students
- All students, regardless of sexual orientation, reported the lowest levels of depression, suicidal feelings, alcohol and marijuana use, and unexcused absences from school when they were
    - In a positive school climate and
    - Not experiencing homophobic teasing.

(Retrieved from
http://www.cdc.gov/lgbthealth/youth.htm)

While school related behaviors and attitudes are traumatic, issues and attitudes in the home are even more so. Ryan, Huebner, Diaz and Sanchez (2009), found significantly higher rates of mental and physical health problems among LGBTQ young adults who experienced high levels of rejection from their parents at home while they were adolescents. When compared with LGBT young adults who experienced very little or no parental rejection, LGBTQ young adults who experienced high levels of rejection were for found to be nearly 6 times as likely to have high levels of depression, more than 8 times as likely to have attempted suicide, 3 times as likely to use illegal drugs, and more than 3 times as likely to engage in unprotected sexual behaviors that put them at increased risk for HIV and other sexually transmitted infections.

Early Adolescence

Adolescence is the longest period in the developmental cycle encompassing ages 12 to 24. In fact it took us twelve years or so to reach this stage and we will spend the next twelve years of our life in this stage. There are however three very distinct phases of adolescence which will help us to understand the myriad of challenges developing youth face. The first is ***early adolescents ages 12-15***. As a young person grows and gets older, there are many physical changes that take place.

This is the stage we refer to as puberty. In early adolescence, females begin growing pubic hair, breasts start developing and menstruation may start. Males experience sudden growth spurts, begin to notice the deepening of their voice, and light hair developing on the face, legs, chest and pubic areas. There is no real consistency in the age in which these changes may begin. Generally, puberty starts earlier in girls than in boys. Further, some may begin to show physical changes early while others don't experience them until the latter end of this phase.

The social aspects and relations are very important in the development of early adolescents. Peer pressure is a common problem among this age group. As peers are truly the *only* people to understand the early adolescent and what they are experiencing, pressures to do things such as having sexual relations, drugs, tobacco, and alcohol and other risk taking behaviors can be very strong. There is a tremendous pressure to fit in and be popular.

This pressing and urgent need can and does cause early adolescents to change the way they eat, dress, talk or act. All teens want to fit in. This *fitting in* helps one to understand and ultimately define an identity for themselves, at first separate from their *big people* and later (as the mature through late adolescents), from the peer group to truly form a "self" identity. So try as we may *big people,* we really <u>can't</u> relate to teens. Their world view, manner of communicating, likes, dislikes, interest etc are very different and unique to each generation and each unique peer group.

Once puberty begins, early adolescents experience several hormonal changes. Females produce and release a larger amount of estrogen and males produce and release a larger amount of testosterone. The hormonal surges can cause changes in attitudes, lack of affection and moodiness.

Once stabilized however, hormones can also cause adolescents to have a better sense of right and wrong and higher functioning cognitive and learning skills. Depression is also known to be a common characteristic amongst early adolescents as they try to cope with these changes and to adjust to the shifting body chemistry through hormones.

(Retrieved from http://www.ehow.com/list_6883604_characteristics-early-adolescents.html#ixzz22RVRIFA7)

Figure 50   Early Adolescent

Some of the characteristics that mark early adolescent include:

- Generally ranges from ages 12-15

- Focused on group identity

- Sameness with peer group

- Peer group acceptance

- Still connected to parents, desires direction and advice but on own terms

- Looking to peers for support and like mindedness

- Experimentation & exploration of boundaries.

- Interest and confusion with one's own development

- Physical maturity exceeds social and cognitive skills

- Often critical of personal body features and concerns with physical appearance

- Sex drive!

- Early ♀ or late ♂ physical development leads to teasing and isolation by peers

- Confusion on affinity and relationships because of the here-to-fore social pressure for homo-social relations

The adolescent's primary attachment needs during early adolescence are directed towards peers and often peers mean significantly more to adolescents than family. According to Bowlby (1969), the adolescent is experiencing intense separation attempts and anxiety. As

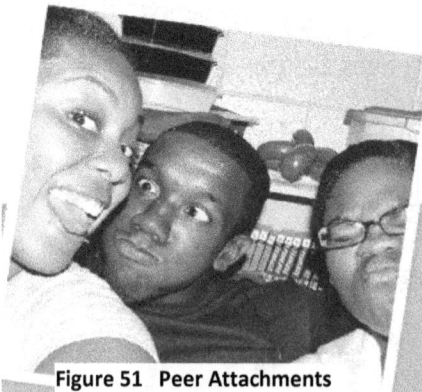

Figure 51 Peer Attachments

the youth grapples with establishing independence, a re-emergence of early separation anxiety occurs.

In addition to the "personal identity", the adolescent is also challenging the establishment of a ***sexual identity*** and in some cases an affirmation of gender identity and sexual orientation. These are not synonymous and should not be confused as such. It is important for us to understand and appreciate the differences. Sex refers to a person's biological status, typically categorized as female, male, or intersex. Intersex is an atypical combination of features that usually distinguish male from female often with secondary sexual organ development of both biological sexes. There are several indicators of one's biological sex, including internal reproductive organs, external genitalia, sex chromosomes, and gonads. All of which comprises our "sex"

Gender alluded to earlier, *is* defined as the feelings, attitudes, and behaviors that a particular culture associates with a person's biological sex. To help clarify why this is a challenge for teens, behavior that is compatible with cultural expectations is referred to as gender-normative; behaviors that are viewed as incompatible with these expectations constitute gender non-conformity and often presents conflict for those that are "non-conforming" ***Gender identity*** is one's sense of oneself as male, female, or transgender. When biological sex and gender identity are not in agreement or congruent, the individual may identify as transsexual or transgender. ***Gender expression*** then is the "...way in which a person acts to communicate gender within a given culture; for example, in terms of clothing, communication patterns and interests. A person's gender expression may or may not be consistent with socially prescribed gender roles, and may or may not reflect his or her gender identity" (Retrieved from http://www.apa.org/pi/lgbt/resources/sexuality-definitions.pdf)

Who you are sexually and romantically attracted is your ***Sexual orientation***. Sexual orientation typically includes attraction to members of the opposite sex (heterosexuals) attraction to members of one's own sex (gay men or lesbians) and attraction to members of both sexes (bisexuals). Contemporary research suggests that sexual orientation does not always appear in such clearly defined categories and instead occurs on a continuum. Further, some research indicates that sexual orientation is fluid for some people. This may be especially true for women. The above categories are however still very typically referred to. Our ***sexual identity*** then consists of all of the above: an individual's sexual orientation, preferences, gender roles, and how they define their individual sexuality. (Retrieved from http://www.apa.org/pi/lgbt/resources/sexuality-definitions.pdf)

Confusing?! Try experiencing it from the perspective of an adolescent. Now I know these are challenging concepts and frankly we all *did* experience them as a teen, but it is very different looking at these experiences from the outside in.

Where as in pre-adolescence, the energy or attraction, (while primarily asexual in nature) was directed towards what I have termed homo-**social** with a hint of 'natural homosexuality', most adolescents direct this new found sexual energy towards the opposite sex. The onset of adolescence is also the onset of dating. Adolescents frequently 'fall in love' and find what they believe are life mates. Most often, these, 'life mates' are little more than short lived crushes.

For some adolescents, this period of sexual exploration and socialization is even more complicated.

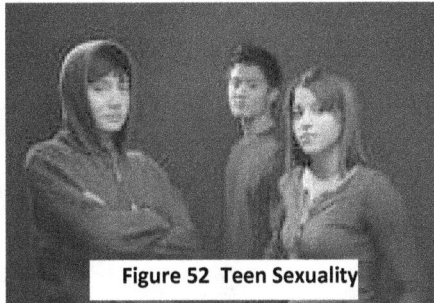
Figure 52 Teen Sexuality

These youngsters are faced with societal pressure to develop heterosexual relationships when they are aware of their own feelings and attractions for members of their own sex. For the gay or bisexual youth, the trauma of adolescence is quadrupled. Add gender identity challenges, gender dysphoria or gender expression experimentation and the trauma of adolescence magnify tenfold. They are bullied, confused, ridiculed and often rejected by peers and family.

Middle Adolescents 15- 18

Entering high school for the mid adolescent brings about renewed anxiety and challenges. A new or enlarged peer group must be formed and for many the challenge of acceptance begins again. By the age of sixteen, many youngsters begin to drive cars, a long awaited first step towards ultimate independence. Many teens begin to shuffle work, school and social life, getting their first taste of 'adulthood'. By seventeen or eighteen, the teen begins to make vital decisions for future life. Decisions about career, college, military, families, etc are

Figure 53 Middle Adolescence

considered during this time.

Cognitively, the adolescent moves into a stage of *Formal Operations* according to Piaget (1952). In this stage, the youth develops the ability for abstract thinking without the necessity of concrete examples. By isolating variables, the youth can solve most any problem. The adolescent can draw conclusions from hypothetical data and can imagine concepts contrary to given facts. The ability to plan realistically for the future begins to emerge and the youngster can begin to grasp and craft metaphors.

By the age of seventeen or eighteen, most physical changes have stabilized and the teen has generally come to grips with their new look and independence. For many, peer groups are well established and peer pressure takes on a less influential role. Many move on to beginning their adult life by working, joining the military or going on to college. These significant changes in life direction do not occur however without some trauma. As the young person leaves high school, he again experiences separation and loss anxiety. She often leaves behind close friends and associates as well as family members.

Later adolescence Ages 18 – 24

At the age of 18 or so (again remember that these ages are all relative) they then enter later adolescence. New challenges for teens surface during late adolescence. Often decisions about career and family have been tentatively made. For those adolescents that enter and complete college or the military, a four year moratorium to "true adulthood' comes to an end. Whereas most college and entry military age folks continue an extended adolescence (all night partying and an intense focus on socializing), by the end of the four year college or enlistment, they are again faced with vital decisions on career and future plans. For some, a bounce back return to home is in order, much to the chagrin of their parents.

Key issues for the late adolescent include:

Figure 54 Late Adolescents

- Individual identity

- "me" ness

- Separation from nest

- The questions of who am I

- The myths of childhood fade

- What do I want to do with my life?

- Peers and a 'new' circle of friends

- Role models for "adult life"

- Life lessons and gaining experience

- Setting off on one's own life course

- College, Trade school, Military, School of hard knocks

Early adulthood 24-34 Years Old

Intimacy vs. Isolation

Erikson (1959) terms the early adult stage as ***intimacy vs. isolation***. Accordingly, this period is identified as the period in which one learns to risk the newly found self-identity to share one's life with close others. It requires an individual to draw upon all previously learned abilities. If an individual does not successfully develop these skills then she will ultimately spend life in isolation with many disruptive or dysfunctional relationships. The theme for this stage of life is ….Love

Somewhere between late adolescence and early adulthood decisions about starting a family, occupations, establishing a home, etc., are typically finalized. Havighurst (1953) outlines several tasks for this age group. Included in his theory are: selecting a mate, learning to live with a partner (married or otherwise), rearing children, managing a home, selecting a congenial social group, maintaining family ties and taking civic responsibilities. Likewise, Levinson (1978), believed that a young adult must master four main tasks:

- He must find a mentor, an older adult that one can look up to, learn from and relate to
- The young adult must also firmly develop a career path

- The establishment of intimacy must be developed
- And finally, the young adult must establish a dream or goal.

More often than not, the young adult's dream or goal is unrealistic or unattainable. The primary purpose for this 'dream' however is to provide inspiration or motivation for growth in the young adult's present activity. As the natural process of maturity occurs, the 'dream' or goal will be redefined more realistically.

Figure 55 Young Family

To provide further clarity on the tasks of the early adult I offer the following:

- How does one enter meaningful relationships without losing the sense of self and identity just developed as an adolescent?

- What framework will one build based on the foundation laid in late adolescence?

- How will one make it in this world?

- How does one manage growing kids if they have entered the picture?

- How does one manage aging parents, aging families?

Figure 56 Young Adult Couple

Gould (1978) believed that the transition into adulthood required the proving of competence as an adult to oneself. As such, the adult begins to surrender the expectation that others will provide continuing assistance and help. The adult should also firmly establish the 'adult relationship' with their parents, in which they no longer 'live just for' the approval of their parents or to meet their parents' expectations for life choices. A process of letting go of old grievances occurs. The adult integrates previous unacknowledged strengths, talents and desires and undergoes a period of re-evaluation and re-dedication to her goals. A cultivation of freely chosen self-interests and values lead to qualities that endure throughout adult life.

Figure 57   Working Young Adults

Middle Adulthood, 34- 60 Years old

Generativity vs. Stagnation

The transition into mid-adulthood (often begun as early as age 30 but typically age 34-60) is a period of settling down. The mid-adult re-commits to his-self as well or may change established patterns. There is a full development of adult autonomy from parents and a process of maintaining an excitement in one's life occurs. This is the period in which one begins to fit her 'dream' firmly into reality. Havighurst (1953) asserts that the mid-adult has achieved social and civic responsibility, has established an economic standard of living and has developed adult leisure activities.

Figure 58   Adult Pondering

Most mid-adults also experience a period of adjustment to changing physiological appearances and abilities. During the mid-life years, ages 34-60, the adult begins to grapple with death, limitations, aging parents, pain, anger, and unfolding dreams. It is again a period of change and introspection. This stage of life brings about a period in which focus is placed by the adult on mentoring others; there is a sense of 'one last chance to do something'. By age 45, there is usually an acceptance of oneself as the final authority and an acceptance that one is fully in charge of his own life. There is a complete assumption of adult consciousness. Erikson (1953) characterizes this stage as generativity vs. stagnation or self-absorption.

Many of the challenges of this stage include:

- Am I doing what I wanted to do?

- Did my life come out as I had planned?

- Have I generated the return I planned?

- Are my kids successful?

- Mid-life crisis

- Can I retire?

- How will I survive on retirement?

- Hey...that didn't hurt yesterday!

- Where did that come from?

- Person you married may not be the person you love now

- Where have the years gone!

Figure 59 Older Adult

- Household changes

- Kids grow up and move

- Your parents may need you

- Physical changes

  - Body can't do what it used to

  - Mind does not remember much of what it once did

  - May need help sleeping, waking, controlling, getting up, getting down, staying up, staying down

- Hormones gone wild

  - One's hormones both male and female begin to change and slow production. Low Estrogen and Low Testosterone begin to wreak havoc on the body.

- Making up for lost time/lost opportunity/ lost life and bad habits

Maslow's quest for self- actualization

The concept of *self actualization* was brought to prominence in Maslow's (1968) *hierarchy of needs* theory and as such is the final level of psychological development that can be achieved when all of one's basic and psychological needs are fulfilled and the "actualization" of a person's full potential is achieved. This concept is offered at this juncture because it is during our mid-adult years that we can dedicate the emotional, physical, psychological, spiritual and material energies to achieving self-actualization.

Maslow (1968) contends that people are aware of their potential and will ultimately do their best to reach the highest levels of creativity and wisdom in the proper environment. That environment is one in which the core or basic needs are satisfied. Further, Maslow shares that the actions of people are not and cannot be dictated simply by the use of stimuli and reinforcement to shape behavior (or forces of mechanical conditioning). Further, they are also not just simply subconsciously controlled by instincts or impulses as thought by most psychoanalysts.

Accordingly, people inherently have basic needs to fulfill, which can be classified into five (5) different levels. These levels are arranged in ascending order, forming a hierarchy that defines which level has to be satisfied before one can move with comfort to the next level. Self actualization resides as the penultimate achievement for human adults. Figure 59 demonstrates Maslow's Hierarchy of Needs. The first level is biological needs and consists of the core physiological requirements of a person to stay alive which includes air, food, shelter and water. These are the strongest and most basic because if a person does not have of any of these, the person will ultimately die.

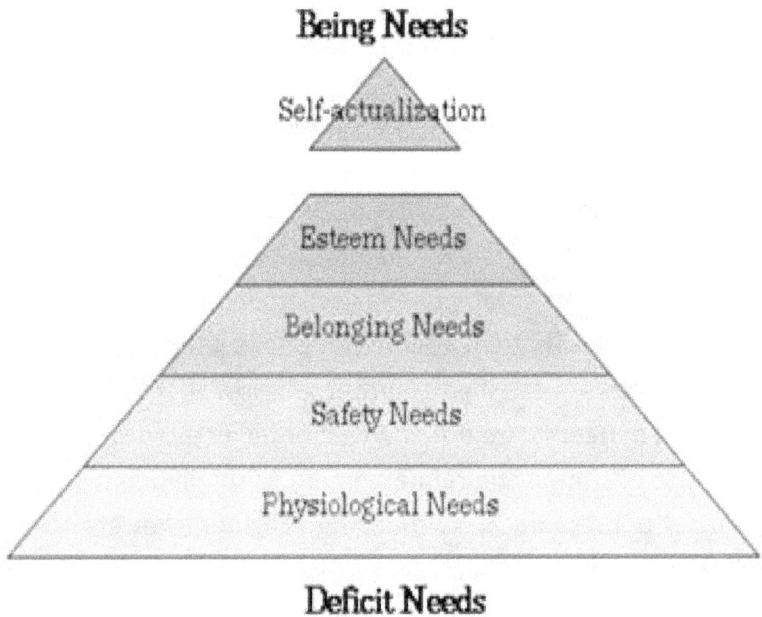

Being Needs

Self-actualization

Esteem Needs

Belonging Needs

Safety Needs

Physiological Needs

Deficit Needs

Figure 60   Maslow's Hierarchy of Needs

These are also the needs that will drive humans into all manner of behavior to achieve. A person who is typically well socially adjusted and a "good citizen" will result to criminal and atypical antisocial behavior to meet these core and basic needs. Safety needs comprise the second level. Once the biological needs of a person are taken care of, the person starts thinking about the need to be safe and secure. Children are far more likely than adults to express this need. The exception of course is in times of emergency, conflict, disaster or social turmoil.

Once one feels safe and secure, they are open to the third level, the need for love, affection, and acceptance by others. This experience opens the door for this person to also want to love, care for, and show acceptance of other people. With normal development, we begin to truly experience this level in our early adult stage once we have become comfortable with our own identity.

As we achieve or become comfortable with the first three levels of the hierarchy, a person begins to seek self-esteem. It is important to note that not everyone who feels that they are loved feels that they are respected. One needs to feel that they are worthy and valuable to others in order to feel genuine self-respect. One must have their basic needs fulfilled, feel that their being and relations are safe and secure and that there is an environment of mutual and true love and affection as the base foundation for feeling respected and ultimately build a level of self-esteem. Without self-esteem, one could feel that he cannot 'do good' for others, for himself, and ultimately ends up lacking the confidence to reach higher goals or for other life successes. Note here that self-esteem is NOT a tangible that can be measured with any level of objective or scientific validity. At best we can measure using subjective reports and anecdotal reference on how one 'feels' about themselves and perhaps have some quantifiable measurement or scale that reflects relative movement based on circumstantial reports.

Self-actualization is the highest and final level in Maslow's hierarchy of needs. Note the gap between this level and the base levels in Figure 59. That gap symbolizes the relative difficulty in achieving this level over the others. This level is in fact the most difficult to achieve. Maslow(1968) suggests that self-actualization is a ongoing process; thus the things or experiences that satisfy the needs in the first four levels are easier to identify, self actualization requires deep introspection on the part of the person before one knows how to satisfy the quest.

Self-actualization is the ability to do something that renders our life complete, a cause, a mission or calling, a vocation or other form of achievement. Most often, in my experience, self- actualization entails some manner of spiritual evolution and encounter. It has also been achieved concurrently with some type of profound life challenge, an illness, near death or significant crisis that helps put life in perspective. Maslow holds that without self-actualization, a person's voyage towards full satisfaction is never quite complete.

To this extent, the following ***Characteristics of a Self Actualized Person, the realization of one's potential*** are offered:

- Openness to experiences:

    - Unafraid of the unknown

    - Less of a need to impose in advance a rigid structure upon experience

    - The result of such openness
        - less anxiety,
        - more flexible (able to roll with the punches)
        - more efficient perception of self, self needs and the developing situation

- Self Confidence:

    - Not incapacitated by excessive guilt, anxiety or fears of inadequacy.

    - The result of Self Confidence:

        - Does not waste energies on unnecessary concern for the approval of others or in seeking to avoid other people's disapproval or rejection

- Sincerity:

  - Most often act on the basis of their own principles and perceived needs, rather than on the basis of facades or pretended selves.

  - Interactions are characterized by honesty, candidness, genuineness, transparency, and authenticity

  - The result of sincerity:

    - Personal experience, personal awareness and interpersonal communication tend to be congruent,

    - No need to hide behind defenses.

- Integration:

  - There is internal interrelation between intellect and emotion

  - The result of Integration:

    - Potentially "unacceptable" thoughts and feelings are not disowned or denied but examined and come to terms with.

- Simplistic dichotomies and polarities
  are unneeded and therefore dissolved

- Ability to love:

  - Have the capacity for forming deeper, more
    uninhabited relationships with others

  - The main issues are not *being loved* by
    someone but rather **developing the capacity to
    love others and one 's self.**

  The result of the ability to love:

    - Greater capacity for empathy and
      mutual dialogue,

    - Richer far more satisfying love and sex
      life.

- Democratic character structure:

  - Emphasizes two-way dialogue and negotiated
    problem solving (win-win)

  - No need to power or status trip others

  - Willing to learn from anyone of suitable
    character

  - he Results of a democratic character structure:

- The ability to get along with many varieties of people

- No evidence of sadomasochistic, codependent interpersonal relations.

Maslow recommends the following steps to help one achieve personal growth and thus, hopefully, self-actualization:

1st be authentic and aware of your own inner feelings;

2nd transcend your cultural conditioning and be a citizen of the 'world';

3rd help yourself discover your true vocation in life; and

4th teach yourself to realize that life is precious and worth living, and that there are joys to be experienced in life.

Following the above steps and striving to master the characteristics listed above will move you close to the pinnacle of self-actualization. It is noteworthy that this is a process and a part of a longer journey as alluded to before; there is a certain spiritual component implied and inherent in this quest.

Later Adulthood ages 60-75

Integrity vs. Despair

The entry into late adulthood at age 60 brings on a stage of self-reflection. The **later adult** begins to adjust to decreasing physical strength and health, begins to consider or in-fact does retire, and must often adjust to the death of a spouse or peers. According to Erikson (1953), the **integrity vs. despair** stage presents the adult with questions such as: 'was my life worthwhile?' The adult reflects on life choices to determine if she made appropriate and meaningful selections. A positive response brings on an inner peace, whereas a negative response brings on a sense of despair or a feeling of purposelessness.

As the adult continues to age she begins to be concerned with comfortable retirement and living arrangements. He has more time to devote to enjoyable activities and leisure. Focus on mentoring younger adults is renewed as civic and social responsibility take on a more significant role. Most older adults take great pride in their sagely knowledge and experience and are more than willing to share with younger seekers. The assumption of expanded civic and social responsibilities often accompanies retirement. As most late adults look forward to retirement, more often than not, they become bored with all the free time and seek additional activity to occupy their time.

Unfortunately, for many retirement age adults in America, retirement often means extremely harsh living conditions on fixed incomes. For many, the retirement years are not as enjoyable as the senior must work to survive. High medical bills or insurance costs, fixed incomes, limits on income amounts, and outrageous taxes combine to make what should be an enjoyable retirement a virtual nightmare. For most, retirement is the culmination of a lifetime of experiences. If the senior had adjusted well to other life changes, retirement should present few significant problems. If not, retirement can be as traumatic as adolescence.

As the aging process continues, the older adult begins to adjust to limited mobility, declining health, the loss of loved ones and isolation. There is a strong force towards self-awareness as the older adult begins to consider their own death. A pass-in-review of one's life occurs as the adult struggles to resolve any remaining issues.

Some of the most profound challenges of this stage include:

- Retirement

    - Sedentary vs. active

    - Useful vs. in-the-way

- Second or third career

- Waning physical and mental facilities and reduced capacity

    - For driving

    - For self mobility

    - For self care

- Fixed income

    - Medications

    - Health care

    - No personal savings

        - Loss of company retirement plans/pensions

        - Declining social security income

- Aged family, home, communities

- Life in review

Figure 61 illustrates both the rewards of later adulthood and the challenges we may face.

Figure 61 Adults in later life

"He who is of a calm and happy nature will hardly feel the pressure of age, but to him who is of an opposite disposition, youth and age are equally a burden." -- Plato (427-346 B.C.)

Very old age – Elderhood age 75 till death

Immortality vs. extinction ...the golden years

Newman & Newman (2012) refer to the last stage of life as Elderhood. Elderhood in this context refers to those individuals who have lived past the typical life expectancy of their peers. As such, Newman and Newman (2012) suggest that there are two different types of people described in this stage of life. 1st The "young old" are those healthy individuals who continue to function on their own without assistance and 2nd The "old old", those who are dependent on specific services as a result of declining health or diseases. We refer to this period of life is characterized as a period of "***immortality vs. extinction***." Immortality this, is the belief that your life will go on past death, some examples are an afterlife or living on through ones family. Extinction is the feeling that one's life had no purpose. There are many individuals that have lived past all family and friends and feel a great loss I have seen these folks as bitter and distraught residents in nursing homes and the like.

Some findings of the Pew Research Center indicate that among respondents ages 65 to 74, a third say they feel 10 to 19 years younger than their actual age, and one-in-six say they feel at least 20 years younger than their actual age. These folks would be an example of the "young old". This population is amongst the older adults who have a *"count-my-blessings"* attitude when asked to look back over their lives. The study further reveals that nearly half (45%) of adults ages 75 and older believe that their life turned out better than expected, while just 5% say it has turned out worse (the remainder say things have turned out the way they expected or have no opinion).

There are certainly some downsides to aging and many of these issues trigger depression or lack of motivation for the aged:

- About one-in-four adults ages 65 and older report
    - experiencing memory loss.
- About one-in-five say they
    - have a serious illness,
    - are not sexually active, or
    - often feel sad or depressed.
- About one-in-six report
    - they are lonely or
    - have trouble paying bills.
- One-in-seven cannot drive.
- One-in-ten say they feel they aren't needed or are a burden to others.

Retrieved from http://www.pewsocialtrends.org/2009/06/29/growing-old-in-america-expectations-vs-reality/

Of the most challenging aspects of aging is the general physical decline and becoming less active.

As articulated in the above statistics, aging, amongst other things can cause:

- Hair loss
- Change of hair color to gray or white
- Wrinkles and liver spots on the skin due to loss of subcutaneous fat
- Reduced circulatory system function and blood flow
- Reduced immune system function
- Greater susceptibility to bone and joint diseases such as osteoarthritis and osteoporosis
- Reduced lung capacity
- Changes in the vocal cords that produce the typical "old person" voice
- Depression
- Weakened hearing
- Diminished eyesight
- Reduced mental/cognitive ability.
- Memory Loss is common due to the decrease in speed of information being encoded, stored, and received. It may take more time to learn new information.
- Lessening or cessation of sex, sometimes because of physical symptoms such as erectile dysfunction in men, but often simply a decline in libido also known as sex drive.

- Dementia or Alzheimer's related behavioral changes including
  - wandering,
  - physical aggression, and
  - verbal outbursts due to diseases such as depression, psychosis, or dementia.

This final stage in the human development experience is summarized with the following:

- A Complete pass in review

- One may have outlived family and in some cases ones on offspring

- Questions such as

  - "what legacy will I leave?"

  - "did my life have meaning?"

  - "has life passed me by?"

- A feeling of resolve

- Being at peace with mortality

- A personal sunset

- Profound WISDOM

Moral development

Our understanding of moral development will come from the work of Lawrence Kohlberg (1927-1987) Kohlberg offers three levels divided into six stages. The first level of moral thinking referred to as Pre-conventional is equated generally to the pre-elementary school ages. In the first stage of this level, people behave according to socially acceptable norms because they are told to do so by some big person or authority figure (e.g., parent or teacher). We behave because of the threat of punishment. The second stage of this level is characterized by the notion that "good" behavior means acting in one's own best interests or that by doing so, we will receive a reward. This level is referred to as hedonistic morality.

Figure 62 Moral development

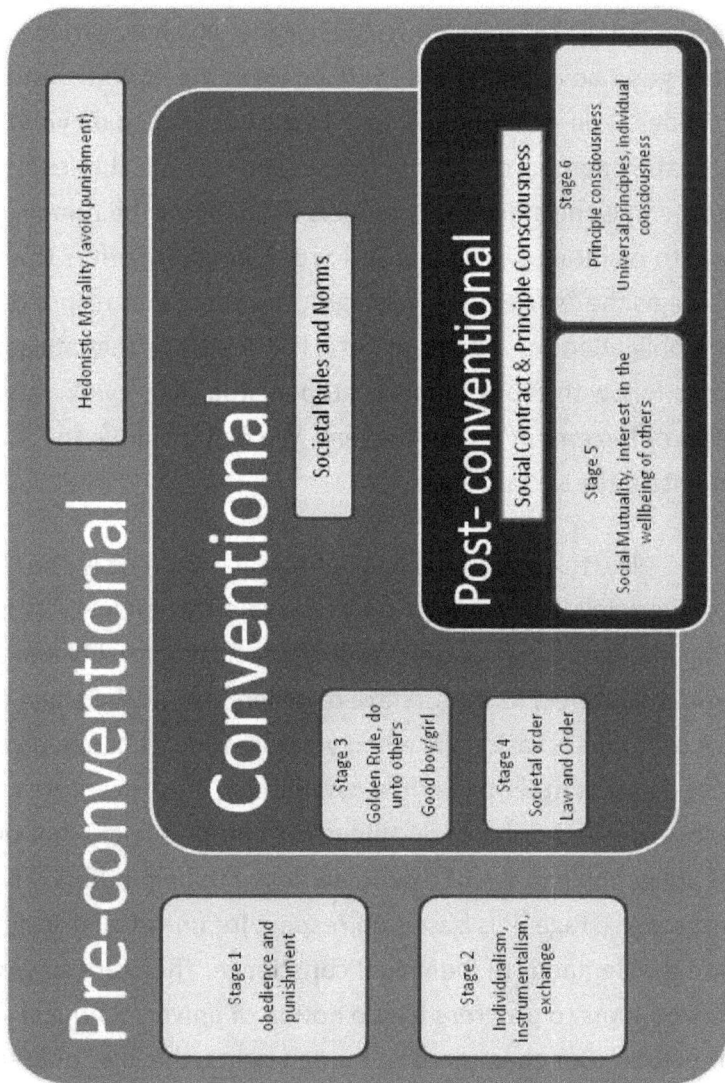

Stages of Moral development

Pre-conventional
- Hedonistic Morality (avoid punishment)
  - Stage 1: obedience and punishment
  - Stage 2: Individualism, instrumentalism, exchange

Conventional
- Societal Rules and Norms
  - Stage 3: Golden Rule, do unto others / Good boy/girl
  - Stage 4: Societal order / Law and Order

Post-conventional
- Social Contract & Principle Consciousness
  - Stage 5: Social Mutuality, interest in the wellbeing of others
  - Stage 6: Principle consciousness / Universal principles, individual consciousness

The second level of morality is that which is generally accepted in society and thus is named "conventional." The first stage of this level (stage 3) is one in which we strive to be "the good boy or good girl" and we learn the notion of the "Golden Rule—Do unto others" that is we seek to do what will gain the approval of others. The second stage of this level (stage 4) is the stage that compels us to follow the rule of law and to maintain simple law and order. Kohlberg offers this stage as the "societal order stage", the stage that responds to the obligations of duty to society. It is the stage that obligates us to follow the speed limit or stop at stop signs even when "law enforcement" is not present. We feel the drive to maintain the social order.

The third and final level of moral reasoning is one that Kohlberg felt is not achieved by the majority of adults. Its first stage (stage 5) is an understanding of social mutuality and a genuine interest in the welfare of others. This is the stage that we drift into occasionally when we donate to a charity, give blood or volunteer to serve a community. This stage takes us above law and order to do things to "better" society, not out of obligation but out of a genuine desire to help others. The last stage (stage 6) is based on respect for universal principle and the demands of individual conscience. There are so very few humans to progress to the notion of universal ethical principles. Our champions of human rights, the likes of Martin Luther King, Mahatma Gandhi, Mother Theresa, Malcolm X,

Nelson Mandela, are the types of individuals that progressed to this level of morality.

Movement through the Moral Stages

Kohlberg's theory of moral reasoning is a stage theory. In other words, we progress through the stages sequentially without skipping any stage. He suggests that people do not automatically move from one stage to the next as they mature. The movement through these stages is not a simple natural flow. Progression from one stage to the next is effected when cognitive dissonance occurs-- that is when a person notices inadequacies in his or her present way of coping with a given moral dilemma. This also implies that one must be cognitively "ready" before moving through a given stage. Further, according to stage theory, one cannot understand moral reasoning more than one stage ahead of their own. For example, a person in Stage 1 can understand Stage 2 reasoning but nothing beyond that. Therefore, we should not expect moral understanding more than one stage ahead of a person's present level of reasoning.

Finally, it is important to note that with moral reasoning is related to the social, psychological, emotional and cognitive development of the individual. As demonstrated in Figure 45 a child in the first level or hedonistic morality has no concept of right or wrong. A toddler of ages one or two, who is still cognitively in Piaget's ***Sensory-Motor*** cannot process the advance concepts of "good boy-good girl". To understand that one's actions have consequences, an individual has to at least be capable of concrete operations—this action equals this consequence. To truly appreciate the inherent good vs. bad of a situation or actions, one <u>must</u> be capable of abstract thought, which implies a level of formal operational thinking, which according to Piaget's theories does not evolve until mid to late adolescents.

Life in balance

The final paradigm to leave you with is one of a life in balance. As we progress to our adult years, we master the challenges articulated through the stages. We must also master living our lives in balance. For this I offer three components for our life that we must strive to balance. Should any one of these components fall out of balance, we must compensate with the others until a homeostasis is returned. Homeostasis is the finite process of achieving and maintaining a balance within a system; in this case, the human system and all of its interactions in a delicate and precise dance.

Our quest to maintain this fine dance epitomizes the human experience. We strive to maintain optimum health, optimum emotional wellbeing and optimum spirit connection, whether that is through an organized religion or simple walks through the park or mountain adventure. To further clarify, should we become physically ill, we must draw heavily upon our emotional self and or spiritual self. Should be wander off too far in to the realm of spirituality; we must be reminded that we do have a physical form and that we must attend to that physical form. Should we become too emotional, we must rely on our spiritual self to keep from reverting to physical force in reaction to our emotionality.

Figure 63   Life Balance

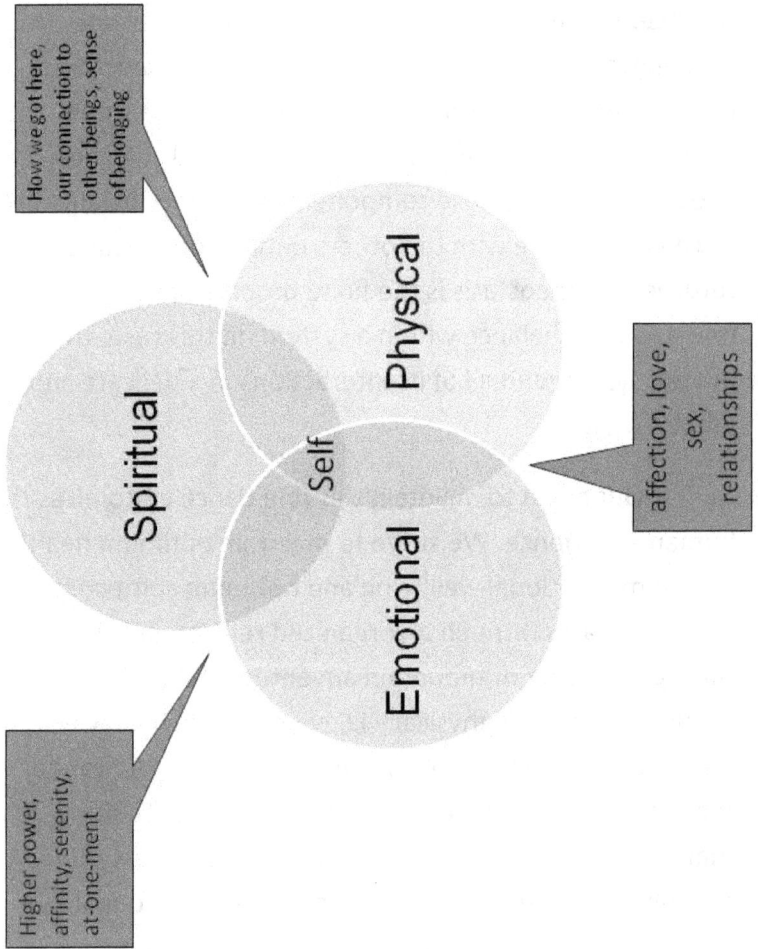

Each of these components is vital to our existence and the balancing alluded to here is vital to our well-being. Much like self-actualization, this balanced life is a quest and a constant process that we endure as we travel through our life span.

Summary

The progression from birth to late adulthood and finally to death is most accurately summarized as a continuing process of growth and change. The individual must struggle to adjust to physiological, psychological, emotional, social and cognitive developmental changes and conflict. The process is painful and enjoyable as well as confusing and exciting at the same time. There are no exacts as each individual develops at separate rates and at separate times. No two individuals develop the same, not even twins. We must each meet our own developmental tasks on our own accord and must achieve resolution through our own resources. One could surmise that the process does not end until we reach our final resolve as earth dwelling beings—death. Through each of the stages, we gain invaluable resources for our "tool" box in which to journey the Human Development Experience.

For the student of human development, it is my hope that this text provides a easy to digest perspective on the subject of developmental theory. For the lay person, I hope this text sparks insights to help you understand the wonderful and exciting world of developmental theory. For all, I hope this text challenges you to study the subject further and to explore the wonderful world of developmental theory and in so doing, move one step closer to being a life-long learner.

Bibliography

Ainsworth, M. (1973). The Development of infant-mother attachment. In B. M. Caldwell, & H. N. Ricciuti, *Review of Child Development Research (Vol. 3)*. Chicago: University of Chicago Press.

American Federation for Suicide Prevention. (2012). *Facts and Figures*. Retrieved 7 22, 2012, from www.asfp.org: http://www.afsp.org/index.cfm?fuseaction=home.viewpage&page_id=050fea9f-b064-4092-b1135c3a70de1fda

American Psychological Association. (2011, February 18). *Sexuality definitions*. Retrieved 8 3, 2012, from APA.org: http://www.apa.org/pi/lgbt/resources/sexuality-definitions.pdf

Bowlby, J. (1988). *Attachment.* New York: Basic Books.

Center for Disease Control and Prevention. (n.d.). *Child Development Positive Parenting*. Retrieved 8 2, 2012, from CDC.gov: http://www.cdc.gov/ncbddd/childdevelopment/positiveparenting/index.html

Centers for Disease Control and Prevention. (UNK). *Lesbian, Gay, Bisexual and Transgender Health*. Retrieved 07 22, 2012, from CDC.gov: http://www.cdc.gov/lgbthealth/youth.htm

Craig, G. (2001). *Human Development.* Englewood Cliffs, N.J.: Pearson College.

Dornbush, S. (. (1988). *Feminism, children and the new family.* New York: Guilford Press.

Ehow.com. (n.d.). *Characteristics of Early Adolescents*. Retrieved 8 2, 2012, from Ehow.com: http://www.ehow.com/list_6883604_characteristics-early-adolescents.html#ixzz22RVRIFA7

Elements of Behavioral Health. (2012, 7 29). *Domestice Violence Perpetuates the Cycle of Abuse in Children*. Retrieved 7 30, 2012, from Elements of Behavioral Health Creating Extraordinary Lives: http://www.elementsbehavioralhealth.com/mental-health/domestic-violence-perpetuates-cycle-of-abuse-in-children/

Erikson, E. (1950 (rev edition 1993)). *Childhood and society*. New York: Guilford Press.

Erikson, E. (rev. 1994). *Identity, youth and crisis*. New York: Norton.

Erikson, E. (1959). The problem of ego identity. *Identity and Life Cycle: Selected Papers. Psychological Issues Monograph No. 1* .

Frazier, A., & Lisonbee, L. (1950). Adolescent Concerns with physique. *School review, 58* , 397-405.

Freidenberg, E. (1965). *Coming of age in America*. New York: Vantage Books.

Gessell, A. (1940). *The first five years of life: The preschool years*. New York: Harper & Brothers.

Gould, R. (1978). *Transformations, growth and change in adult life*. New York: Simon and Schuster.

Havighurst, R. (1953). *Human Development and education*. New York: Longman.

Jones, W. (1979). Grief and involuntary career change: Its implications for counseling. *Vocational Guidance Quarterly, 27* , 196-201.

Keating, D. (1979). Intellectual talent, research and development. *Hyman Blumberg Symposium in Early Childhood Education.* Baltimore: Johns Hopkins Univesity Press.

Kohlberg, L. (1966). Moral education in schools: A developmental review. *School Review, 74* , 1-30.

Kohlberg, L. (1963). The development of children's orientations toward moral order. I : Sequences in the Development of Moral Thought. *Vita Humana, 6* , 11-35.

Levinson, D. (1978). *The seasons of a man's life.* New York: Knopf.

Lewis, M., Rosenblum, L., & (ed). (1974). *The effects of infants on it's caregiver.* New York: Wiley.

Mandler, G. (1984). *Mind and body: Psychology of Emotion and Stress.* New York: W.W. Norton.

Marcia, J. (1980). Identity in adolescents. In J. Adelson, *(ed) Handbook of Adolescent Psychology.* New York: Wiley.

Maslow, A. (1999). *Toward a Psychology of Being.* New York: Wiley.

Mead, G. H., & (Ed) Deegan, M. J. (2001). *Play, scholl and Society.* New York: Peter Lang Publishing.

Muuss, R. (1962). *Theories of Adolescence.* New York: Random House.

Neimark, E. (1975). Intellectual development during adolescence. In F. H. ed, *Review of Child Development (vol 4)*. Chicago: Univesity of Chicago Press.

Newman, B., & Newman, P. (2012). *Development through life*. Belmont: Wadsworth.

Peters, M. (1981). Parenting in Black Families with young children. In H. McAdoo, & J. McAdoo, *(eds) Black Children*. Beverly Hills: Sage.

Pew Research Center. (unk). *Growing Old in America Expectations vs. Reality*. Retrieved 8 10, 2012, from Pew Social Trends: http://www.pewsocialtrends.org/2009/06/29/growing-old-in-america-expectations-vs-reality/

Piaget, J. (1972). Intellectual evolution from Adolescence to adulthood. *Human Develpment Vol. 15* , 1-12.

Piaget, J. (1952). *The origin of intelligence in children, M. Cook, Trans.* New York: International University Press.

Piaget, J. (1950). *The psychology of intelligence, M. Percy & D.E. Berlyne, trans.* New York: Harcourt.

Prevention, A. F. (2012). *Facts and Figures*. Retrieved 7 22, 2012, from www.asfp.org: http://www.afsp.org/index.cfm?fuseaction=home.viewpage&page_id=050fea9f-b064-4092-b1135c3a70de1fda

Prevention, C. f. (UNK). *Lesbian, Gay, Bisexual and Transgender Health*. Retrieved 07 22, 2012, from CDC.gov: http://www.cdc.gov/lgbthealth/youth.htm

Ryan, C., Huebner, D., Diaz, R. M., & Sanchez, J. (2009). Family rejection as a predictor of negative health outcomes in white and Latino lesbian, gay, and bisexual young adults. *Pediatrics vol. 123* , 346-353.

Sheehy, G. (1974). *passages: Predictable Crises of Adult Life.* New York: Bantam.

Sorenson, R. (1973). *Adolescent sexuality in contemporary America: Personal Values and Sexual Behavior ages 13-19.* New York: World.

Spanier, G. (1977). Sexual socialization: A Concpetual Review. *Journal of the Family Vol. 6* , 121-146.

Wermke, K. (2009, 11 09). *Science Daily, Science News: Babies' Language Learning Starts From The Womb.* Retrieved 07 04, 2012, from Science Daily.com: http://www.sciencedaily.com/releases/2009/11/091105092607.ht m

Wilie, C. (1976). *A new look at Black Families.* Bayside: General Wall.

Worden, J. (1982). *Grief Counseling and grief therapy: A handbook for the mental health practitioner.* NewYork: Springer.

www.ingramcontent.com/pod-product-compliance
Lightning Source LLC
Chambersburg PA
CBHW061747270326
41928CB00011B/2413